I0820574

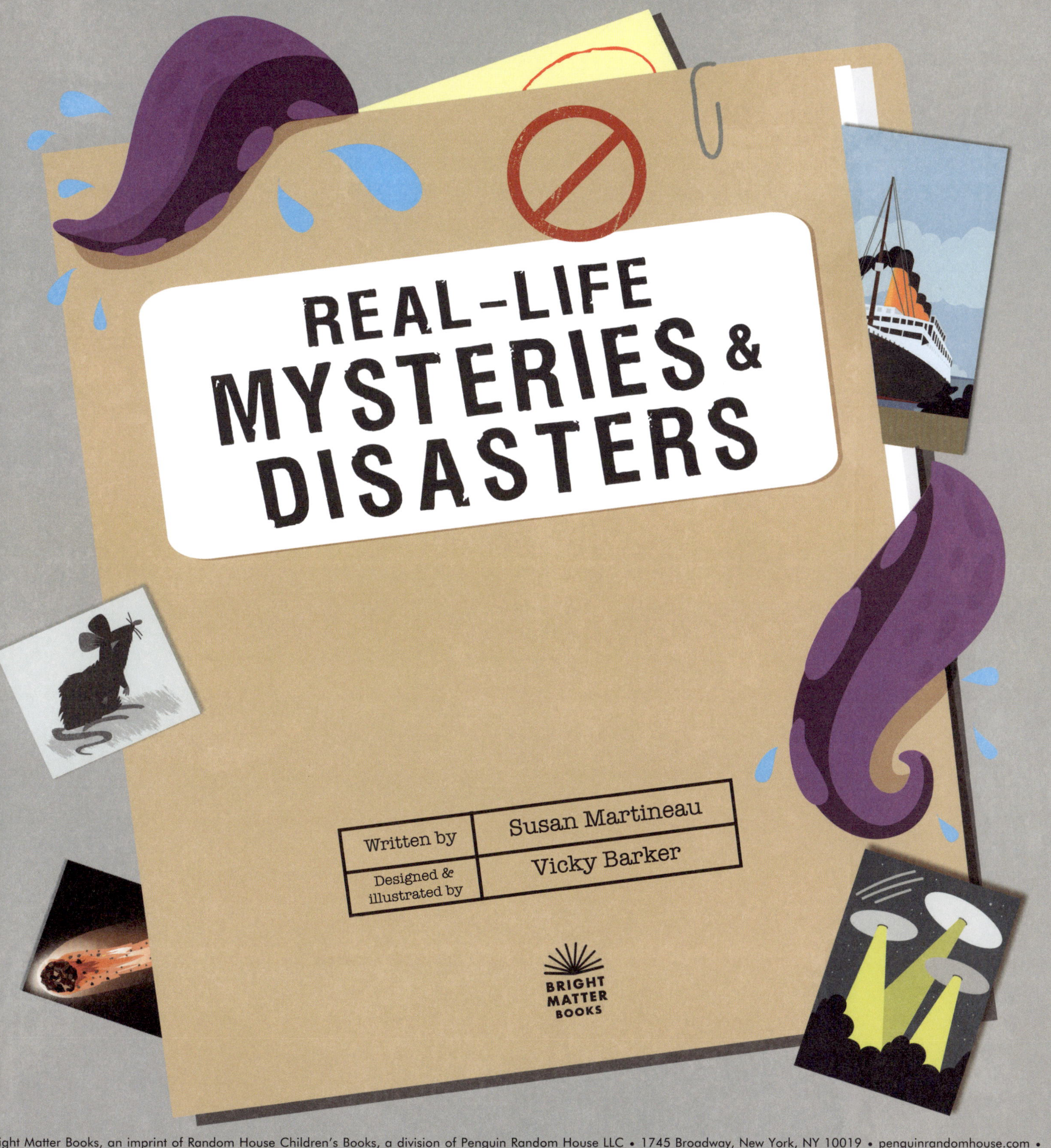

right Matter Books, an imprint of Random House Children's Books, a division of Penguin Random House LLC • 1745 Broadway, New York, NY 10019 • penguinrandomhouse.com •
ncbooks.com • • Library of Congress Cataloging-in-Publication Data is available upon
equest. • ISBN 979-8-217-11630-0 (trade) — ISBN 979-8-217-11631-7 (ebook) • Originally published in the United Kingdom by b small publishing ltd. in 2017 and 2020 • The authorized
epresentative in the EU for product safety and compliance is Penguin Random House Ireland, Morrison Chambers, 32 Nassau Street, Dublin D02 YH68, Ireland, http://eu-contact.penguin.ie.
Random House Children's Books supports the First Amendment and celebrates the right to read. • Manufactured in China • 10 9 8 7 6 5 4 3 2 1

PART 1: REAL-LIFE MYSTERIES

PART 2: REAL-LIFE DISASTERS

PART 1
REAL-LIFE MYSTERIES
CAN YOU EXPLAIN THE UNEXPLAINED?

CASE FILE
Real-Life Mysteries

Everyone loves a good mystery! Here are some of the most intriguing cases of all time. Many people have tried to find the truth behind them, but these mysteries are not so easily solved.

Read the amazing stories first. Then look at the CASE FILE for each one so that you can examine the evidence so far. Will YOU be the one to uncover the truth?

INVESTIGATING THE UNEXPLAINED

Keep an open mind and your wits about you. Try to look carefully and objectively at the facts. It is easy to get carried away imagining all sorts of things that might hide the truth.

The aim of any investigation is to find proper evidence.

WITNESSES

Interview people who say they have had an unusual or spooky experience. You could record what they say and write it up afterward.

Being OBJECTIVE means to make up your mind by looking at facts rather than being guided by emotions or feelings!

LOCATIONS

If you plan to visit a place where mysterious things have happened, make sure you do not go alone and always ask permission from an adult.

INVESTIGATOR'S KIT

Always keep a notebook and pen with you so that you can keep careful notes and draw diagrams if necessary.

EVIDENCE

Prepare your facts and findings so that you can present them to your friends and family. They will be fascinated.

Mystery Word

There is a full list of mystery words and other related terms on the final page of this book.

pseudoscience

inexplicable

READ the files.

EVALUATE the evidence. And DECIDE what *you* think really happened!

The Legend of Bigfoot

In 1967 two ranchers, Roger Patterson and Bob Gimlin, were riding through Bluff Creek in California. They saw a large, ape-like creature crouching by the river. As they rode toward it, the huge beast stood up on its hind legs and the men could see it was covered in dark fur. As it strode away into the trees Patterson managed to film it, despite being thrown to the ground by his terrified horse.

This was not the first time such a creature had been seen in the vast forests of North America. Even people who were used to being out there in the big woods had been scared by the man-ape called Bigfoot or Sasquatch.

The name Sasquatch comes from a Salishan word meaning "wild man." Each Native American tribe had its own name for this gigantic creature.

Hunters and trappers in the 1800s told tales of massive footprints that looked oddly human. There were sightings of immensely tall creatures covered in dark hair, with very long arms and small heads, no neck, and huge shoulders.

Monster Word

cryptozoology

is the study of animals that remain hidden (cryptids). They may or may not exist!

More blood-curdling still were stories of people being kidnapped or attacked by groups of Sasquatch. Country folk living in remote log cabins reported being terrorized by something unspeakable prowling outside. They would hear yowling and bizarre whistling noises unlike any other animal they had ever heard. It also had a foul smell!

The stories of sightings have never really stopped to this day. Many people in the northern areas of America and Canada have come forward to tell of their own encounters with Bigfoot in forests, in their backyards, or along remote country roads. Can they all be mistaken or lying? What is the truth behind BIGFOOT?

Turn over to read the **case file** notes . . .

CASE FILE: Bigfoot
The evidence so far . . .

Turn back to read the stories behind the case file.

Bluff Creek Video

The film taken in 1967 by Roger Patterson shows the creature turning to look at him and walking rapidly into the woods.

 Is it just someone in a gorilla suit?

 The Disney film company said at the time that it would have been very difficult and expensive to fake the movements of the animal.

Photos

A large number of these exist. Most of them are pretty blurry, but the people who took them were shocked and scared.

No bones or bodies have ever been found!

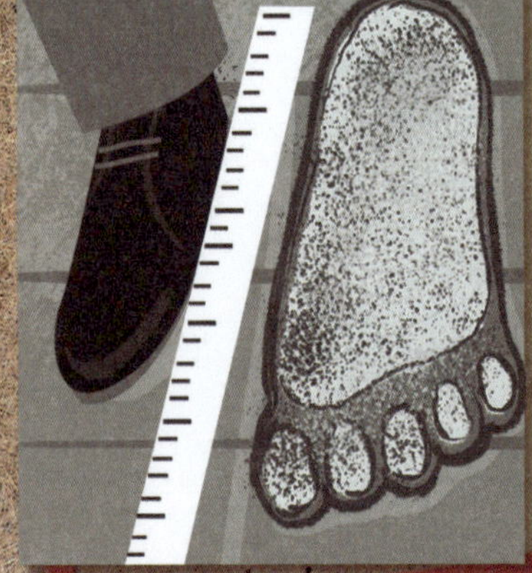

Giant Footsteps

Many Sasquatch footprints have been found over the years and plaster casts have been taken of some of them.

 It is easy to fake these and some people have even admitted to making enormous wooden feet to produce joke prints.

 But some Bigfoot tracks are so detailed that "fingerprints" (or dermatoglyphs) can be seen. These are very hard to fake.

Witness Statements

There is a long history of sightings. Does this make it more likely that there is some truth to them?

"My first impression was of a huge man, about six feet tall, almost three feet wide . . . covered from head to foot with dark brown silver-tipped hair."

William Roe, highway worker, 1955

"I am not entirely sure what I saw that day but I know it was not a bear and it was not a human."

14-year-old boy out hunting, 1990

Newspapers and the internet mean that Bigfoot stories can be spread all around the world. Maybe some people might make up a sighting to have their fifteen minutes of fame?

Bigfoot Identikit

Height:
6 to 10 feet (1.8 to 3 meters)

Shoulders:
3 feet (90 cm) wide

Fur:
dark brown or reddish brown, none around mouth and eyes

Head:
conical, with ears on side

Feet:
1 to 1.8 feet (30 to 55 cm) long

Main Theories

Bigfoot is a kind of human. Could it be a "missing link" between primitive humans and us?

Bigfoot is a bear. But bears don't generally walk on hind legs and their ears are on top of their heads.

Bigfoot does not exist!

Bigfoot is related to a type of giant ape called Gigantopithecus that died out 100,000 years ago.

Alma
Mongolia or Russia

Yeti
Himalayas

Yeren
China

Orang Pendek
Sumatra

Yowie
or "Big Fellah"
Australia

Location

Mainland Canada and USA, but most often in the vast, deep forests of the Northwest regions, where there are plenty of hiding places for a mysterious beast.

Further Investigations

Other forms of ape-men or "wild men" to find out about.

Camp out in the woods if you dare!

Versailles Time-Slip

On a hot August day in 1901, two English women were visiting the palace of Versailles near Paris. Charlotte Moberly and Eleanor Jourdain were walking in the palace grounds near a smaller chateau called the Petit Trianon.

Charlotte and Eleanor had lost their way when they started to notice that all the other people in the gardens were dressed in old-fashioned costumes. The atmosphere felt flat and heavy. They saw two men in strange uniforms . . .

. . . and Charlotte noticed there was a woman in a beautiful dress sitting sketching among the trees. When they returned from their walk, they were astonished to learn that no one else had seen anyone dressed in an old style or a lady drawing that day.

They began to suspect that they had somehow seen a scene from the past. When they returned to the gardens, they saw many new details and curious features, but they could not find a small bridge they had crossed the first time.

Charlotte and Eleanor were so intrigued by their experience that they published a book about what they had seen. They concluded that they had witnessed a version of the palace and gardens dating from the late 1700s. They thought that the lady sketching must be none other than the doomed queen consort of France Marie Antoinette, who was executed in 1793.

Other people also claim to have observed strange things in the Versailles gardens and to have felt an unpleasant heaviness and gloom. There have also been more reports of a "sketching lady" near the Petit Trianon and sightings of people dressed in the fashions of the eighteenth century.

Were they all just imagining things, or could it be that they experienced a view into the past?

Spooky Word

apparition

The strange and unexpected appearance of someone or something.

Turn over to read the **case file** notes . . .

CASE FILE: Versailles Time-Slip

The evidence so far . . .

Turn back to read the story behind the case file.

Location

The Petit Trianon and its gardens were where the eighteenth-century French queen Marie Antoinette used to go to get away from the main court of the palace of Versailles.

The gardens are full of winding paths, curious buildings, and mysterious little glades. It is easy to get lost here!

The Evidence

There are no photos or any film footage of this incident. The evidence is in the form of witness statements by Moberly and Jourdain.

Witness Statements

Moberly and Jourdain's book about their experience was called An Adventure. It was published in 1911, ten years after their trip to Versailles. The women did not use their real names as the authors.

In 1958 a researcher named Guy Lambert said that the two women had indeed described the Petit Trianon as it would have appeared around 1770.

Witness Reliability

Charlotte Moberly was the principal of a college at Oxford University and Eleanor Jourdain was a headmistress. They would seem to be honest witnesses, but let's consider:

- Might they have seen old pictures of how the Petit Trianon and the gardens looked in the 18th century before their visit?
- Why did they wait so many years before publishing their book?
- Why did they not use their real names as the authors when the book was first published?

Main theories

The women experienced what is called a **time-slip**, which meant they could "tune into" the past. Perhaps time-slips are more likely in places where important historical events have happened?

The people in old-fashioned dress were at a costume party or historical reconstruction in the gardens. In this case their costumes were extremely accurate. The men in uniform looked exactly like the Swiss Guards who protected Marie Antoinette.

A mysterious place, like these gardens, might lead you to imagine something intriguing. Then the more you tell the story, the more you believe you've seen something strange!

Further Investigations

Some ghost stories describe the apparition "floating" along the ground. Is this a "time-slip"? The ground might have been higher and less worn-down in the past.

Tell your friends an interesting story. Then ask them to tell it back to you a week later. See if it's the same story!

Unidentified Flying Objects

In 1947 a pilot named Kenneth Arnold was flying over Mount Rainier in Washington when he saw some strange crescent-shaped aircraft moving incredibly fast.

Arnold described the objects as flying like a saucer would if you skimmed it across the water. Newspaper reports then called them "flying saucers," and this name has been used to describe many **UFOs (Unidentified Flying Objects)** since.

During the 1970s many people reported seeing large triangular aircraft moving slowly and silently across the sky. These mysterious objects were seen mainly in England and Europe. They did not look like any aircraft ever seen before.

In 1974, people in Llandrillo, Wales, were frightened by a massive explosion and rumbling sound. They could also see bright lights moving quickly across the night sky. Army officials soon appeared on the scene, and stories spread that a UFO had crashed on a nearby mountain. It was rumored that its alien passengers had been taken away in secrecy by the army.

In 1978 in New Zealand, strange lights were spotted in the skies off the coast of Kaikoura. Air traffic controllers could not identify them as any known aircraft. Many anxious people called the local police as they could see powerful beams of light being projected onto the sea from the craft.

Cargo plane spots strange lights.

These are just a very few of the thousands of stories told about UFOs. What are these objects, and where do they come from?

Cases of Unidentified Weird Lights

Hessdalen Lights

Yellowish, bullet-shaped lights and small red dots were seen in the sky in a remote region of Norway in the 1980s. Investigators flashed a laser beam at one light and it seemed to send answering flashes.

Sea Lights

For centuries sailors have reported seeing swirling wheels of light below the surface of the sea in the Persian Gulf and Indian Ocean. The wheels sometimes appear to rise spookily above the water.

Foo Fighters

Mysterious balls of light were seen in the skies by World War II fighter pilots in the 1940s. These unidentifiable lights would fly near or alongside their aircraft.

Turn over to read the **case file** notes . . .

CASE FILE: UFOs

The evidence so far . . .

Turn back to read the stories behind the case file.

WITNESSES
Thousands of people all over the world.

Key Witness

Kenneth Arnold, a pilot who first described UFOs as "flying like a saucer." He became the world's first private UFO investigator. He interviewed many other people who claimed to have seen strange flying objects in the sky.

An FBI officer interviewed Kenneth Arnold and stated: *"It is the personal opinion of the interviewer that he actually saw what he states he saw."*

Time

Modern sightings began with Kenneth Arnold in 1947. Many of the reports date from the era of humans' first space exploration. Perhaps people had spaceships on the brain!

Evidence

There are many photos and videos. These are easy to fake or take from an angle that makes something normal look weird.

The Kaikoura UFOs were captured on film by a journalist on board a cargo plane. You can hear the real fear in the voices of the witnesses on the soundtrack.

Description

Different shapes and forms. After the "flying saucer" label was used, many people said they had seen saucer-shaped UFOs.

Alien Word

ufology

(you-follow-gee)
The study of unidentified flying objects (UFOs)

UFOs are really just aircraft, weather balloons, satellites, or a trick of the light.

Arnold was seeing reflections on his aircraft canopy, missiles, snow flurries, or birds in flight. Arnold totally disagreed with these suggestions.

The flying triangles were stealth bombers and test planes, even though there has never been any official government explanation.

Over 20 different theories were suggested for the Kaikoura sightings, but it is still not known what the UFOs were doing there or where they came from.

Main theories

Could the Llandrillo incident have been an earth tremor or merely hunters with powerful lights? But if so, why did the army appear so quickly on the scene and warn people to stay away?

Conspiracy Theory

Many UFO hunters think that governments around the world are hiding information about UFOs and their alien passengers.

CASE FILE: Lights in the Sky

Hessdalen Lights

Were they caused by something unusual in the rocks of that area? But if that's the case, why did the lights seem to "answer" the laser beam?

Sea Lights

Could they be huge numbers of glowing, phosphorescent sea creatures? But why in a wheel shape? Could they be alien craft under the water?

Foo Fighters

Were these a secret weapon of some sort? If so, strange that they never harmed the fighter planes.

Ancient Alien Astronauts

Is it possible that travelers from other planets visited Earth many thousands of years ago? And did those alien visitors share their knowledge of science and technology with the humans alive then?

Some people believe that, indeed, ancient alien astronauts visited our planet—and that places and objects from that visit still exist. In 1968, an author named Erich von Däniken published a book called *Chariots of the Gods?* in which he put forward some of the amazing ideas below.

Nazca Lines

In the high desert of Peru in South America, there are hundreds of huge shapes on the ground. Some look like animals or humans, but there are also long straight lines running for hundreds of yards. It looks like they are meant to be seen from above. Erich von Däniken suggested that they were landing sites for alien spaceships.

Phaistos Disc

This mysterious disc is engraved with strange symbols in a spiral shape. The disc was found in Phaistos on the island of Crete. It seems to date from thousands of years ago during the time of the ancient Minoan civilization. No one has been able to decipher the symbols completely, and some people say that this is because they are in an alien language.

The Great Pyramid

This is the largest pyramid in Egypt and one of the legendary Seven Wonders of the World. It was probably meant to be a tomb for Pharaoh Khufu (or Cheops). It was built using over two million massive limestone blocks. They fit together so precisely that a knife cannot be pushed between them. How on earth did people who lived so long ago manage to build such a wonder without space-age technology?

Stonehenge

A colossal circle of stones called Stonehenge stands on Salisbury Plain in southern England. The stones are so enormous that it would have been incredibly difficult to move them and put them into position at a time when the wheel had not even been invented. Could it be that Stonehenge is a model of our solar system and that ancient astronauts helped to build it?

Turn over to read the **case file** notes . . .

CASE FILE: Alien Astronauts

The evidence so far . . .

Turn back to read the stories behind the case file.

Stonehenge

Location: England

Age: over 4,500 years

Description: Circle made of huge stones. Some come from Wales, 150 miles (250 km) away, and weigh between 2.5 and 5 tons. The largest stone weighs 30 tons.

This is how Stonehenge might have looked when first built.

Phaistos Disc

Location: Crete

Age: possibly 4,000 years

Description: Clay disc about 6 inches (16 cm) in diameter. Covered in a spiral of stamped symbols on both sides. Some have been decoded but not all.

Nazca Lines

Location: Peru

Age: over 2,000 years

Description: Over 300 patterns including animals such as spiders, birds, and monkeys. Long lines and abstract shapes.

The Great Pyramid

Location: Egypt

Age: about 4,700 years

Description: The biggest of all the pyramids. It is 479 feet (146 meters) high. Contains about 2.3 million blocks of stone. Each weighs over 2.5 tons.

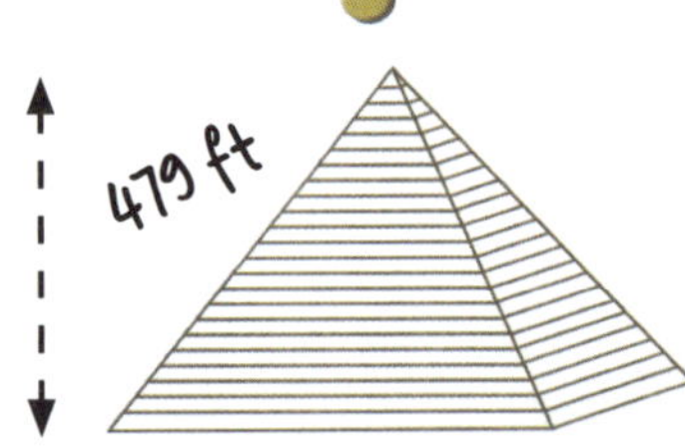

Was Stonehenge an alien building project? Were space travelers building some sort of observatory to watch the stars?

OR

Did prehistoric humans build it using the basic stone tools that archaeologists have discovered at the site? Was it a temple where people gathered to watch the movements of the sun?

Is the Phaistos Disc some kind of alien computer hard drive? The Minoans of Crete were a highly advanced civilization. Did they get their knowledge from travelers from outer space?

BUT

Why would space travelers use a clay disc? It is not very high tech. Archaeologists think that the symbols are probably a Minoan prayer.

Are the Nazca Lines landing sites used by visitors from outer space?

OR

Were they created by the Nazca people, who lived in Peru from about 200 BCE to 500 CE, as a religious site or even some kind of chart of the stars?

Witness Statements

Several books have been published about the idea of aliens visiting Earth long ago. A bestselling book by Erich von Däniken made the idea of ancient astronauts popular.

Von Däniken born 1935.
Worked as hotel manager.
Not a scientist or historian.

Just because something is written in a book does not mean it is true!

Did the ancient Egyptians receive help from space travelers to build this amazing pyramid?

OR

Did they manage perfectly well with their own tools and techniques and thousands of workers?

Reconstruction

Archaeological experiments have succeeded in moving **MEGALITHS** (big stones) using the simple tools that would have been available at the time.

Mystery Word

pseudoscience

Theories about the world that are NOT based on science. "Pseudo" means "false" in Greek.

Curses, Curses, Curses!

Is it possible for something to be cursed or jinxed? Can a ship, a jewel, or a car bring you bad luck?

The Haunted Ship

When the SS *Great Eastern* was launched in 1858, she was the largest ship in the world. The great British engineer Isambard Kingdom Brunel designed her. However, the ship seemed doomed from the start.

Two workmen disappeared during its construction. An accident during the launch killed another workman, and Brunel himself fell seriously ill. Then came the dreadful news that a steam pipe had burst and killed six more men. Poor Brunel died.

The ship was broken up for scrap only 15 years after it was built. As they took it apart the workmen found a gruesome discovery: two skeletons sealed up in the hull. Could the ship have been cursed by the unlucky spirits of those two workmen?

The Jinxed Jewel

There is a mysterious treasure called the Hope Diamond in the Smithsonian Institute in Washington, DC. It is named after one of its many owners.

The diamond is said to have been stolen in the seventeenth century from the eye socket of a temple statue in Myanmar. Since then, it seems to have brought bad luck to many of its owners, including Marie Antoinette, who was executed during the French Revolution in 1793.

Other victims have included a Russian prince who was murdered, a French jeweler who went mad, and a Turkish sultan who killed his wife. The wealthy McLean family of America also suffered tragedy when they owned the jewel. However, the owner named Hope escaped unharmed!

The Cursed Car

James Dean was a young Hollywood actor. On September 30, 1955, he was driving his silver Porsche when he crashed into another car and was killed. He was only 24 years old.

Many of his friends had warned him about this car and said there was something sinister about it. Just a few days before the accident, the actor Alec Guinness warned Dean: "Get rid of that car, or you"ll be dead in a week."

After the accident, the car caused more trouble. It rolled off the back of a truck and crushed the legs of a mechanic. Parts of the vehicle were reused in other cars and all of them were involved in dreadful accidents. While the chassis of the Porsche was being stored in a garage, there was a terrible fire in the building. Weirdly, the car itself was unharmed.

Weird Word

supernatural

A word that describes something that cannot be explained by what we know about the world around us. It comes from the Latin for "beyond nature."

Turn over to read the **case file** notes . . .

CASE FILE: Curses

The evidence so far . . .

Turn back to read the stories behind the case file.

The SS Great Eastern

The Victims

Several workmen.

Brunel himself.

Two workmen vanish and no bodies found until ship is broken up.

The Ship

The biggest steamship of her time.

Nearly 700 feet (210 meters) long and 83 feet (25 meters) wide.

Very expensive to build. The company that built her went bust.

Theories

- Brunel was exhausted by hard work and this may have made him ill.
- The missing workmen were not found, so their deaths jinxed the ship.
- Building such a huge ship was very difficult, and accidents were bound to happen.

The Hope Diamond

The Jewel

A blue Indian diamond about the size of a walnut.

It has had at least 21 owners.

Under certain lights it shines with a blood-red glow.

Ultraviolet light causes this type of diamond to glow red.

The Victims

gone mad

died

committed murder

been murdered

suffered accidents

Some owners have been left unharmed.

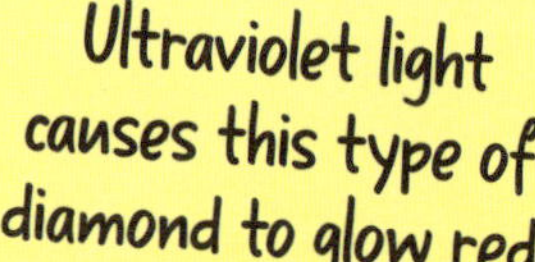

Theories

James Dean's Car

The Car

A silver Porsche 550 Spyder.

The car was designed for racing.

The Victims

James Dean himself.

His passenger survived, but died in another crash years later.

Other racers who reused the car's parts.

Theories

There was something spooky about the vehicle. After the accident it continued to cause trouble for some supernatural reason.

James Dean was driving much too fast. The police had already given him a speeding ticket earlier that day.

The parts of the car that were reused were damaged and should not have been used again.

The odd events that followed the accident were all just strange coincidences.

The Hindu priests of the temple put a curse on the diamond after it was stolen.

What happened to the victims would have happened anyway. A diamond cannot really have caused the French Revolution and the death of the French queen consort.

The story has been exaggerated, by newspapers and in books. Even Evalyn McLean liked to boast that she was wearing a cursed jewel!

Self-Fulfilling Prophecy

This is an interesting theory that says if we *think* something is going to happen, then we might behave in such a way that it actually *does* happen.

Helpful Ghosts

Spectral Sailor

There are many strange and fantastic stories about people in difficulty being helped by a ghostly presence. The famous nineteenth-century yachtsman Joshua Slocum experienced something most unusual on his solo voyage around the world.

As Slocum crossed the North Atlantic in 1895, a huge storm arose, and to make matters worse, he fell ill with terrible stomach pains. Poor, half-fainting Slocum struggled to get back on deck to control his battered boat. As he reached the hatch of his cabin, he felt the boat steady herself and was amazed to see a man in fifteenth-century clothes at the helm.

The stranger introduced himself as helmsman of the *Pinta,* one of the ships used by Christopher Columbus to sail to America in 1492. He reassured Slocum that he would guide the boat while he slept. The boat and Slocum survived to tell the tale!

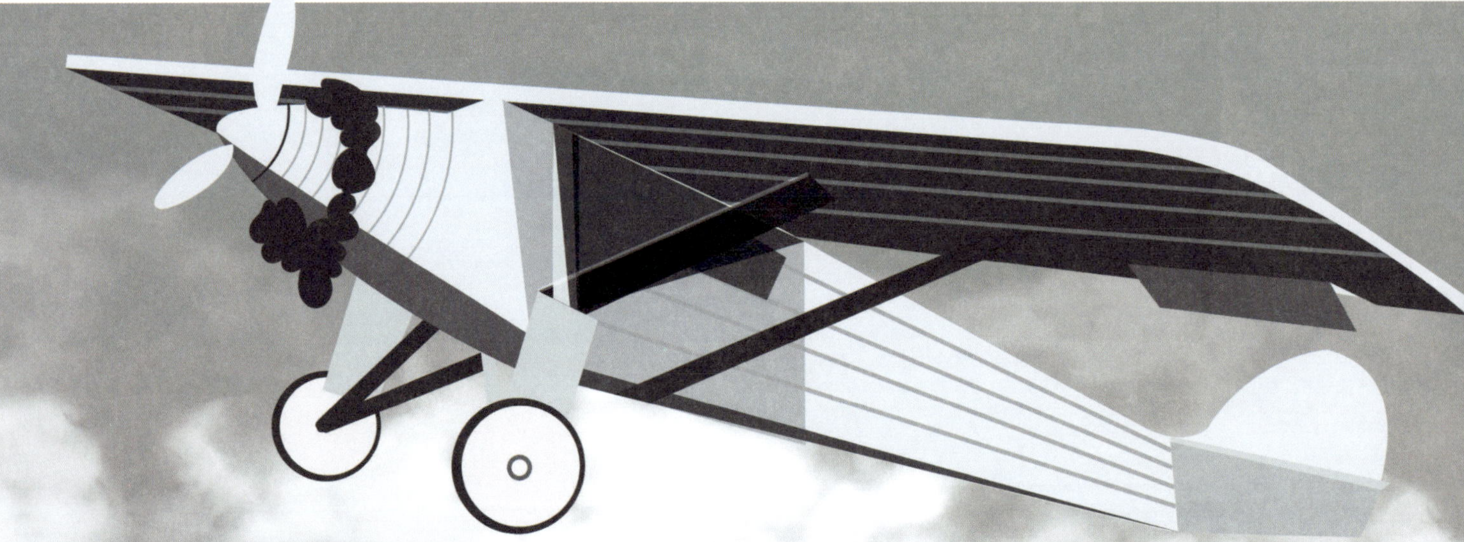

Chatty Phantoms

In May 1927 American aviator Charles Lindbergh was the first person to fly alone and nonstop from New York to Paris. It took him 33 hours. One of his greatest challenges was to stay awake. Afterward he spoke of "phantoms" on board his plane "conversing and advising on my flight."

The Invisible Companion

In 1916 the polar explorers Sir Ernest Shackleton, Frank Worsley, and Tom Crean set off on a terrible trek across the icy mountains on the island of South Georgia, near Antarctica. They were trying to reach a whaling station on the other side of the island to fetch help for the rest of their expedition after their ship had been destroyed by ice.

At the time they did not speak to each other about the uncanny feeling they all had that there was a fourth silent companion on that difficult journey. It was only later that they all admitted that they had felt there was some invisible person there with them who helped them to keep going.

Spooky Space

In 1997 NASA astronaut Jerry Linenger spent five months on board the Russian space station *MIR*. There were many dangerous incidents during this mission, including a serious fire and a near-collision with a supply ship. Jerry says he was aware of the presence of his dead father comforting him and telling him that everything would be all right.

Turn over to read the **case file** notes . . .

CASE FILE: Ghosts

The evidence so far . . .

Turn back to read the stories behind the case file.

Witnesses

Brave, adventurous, and practical people who are used to pushing themselves to their limits. They do not seem like people who would expect to have spooky experiences.

Locations

Extreme places

High altitude in aircraft

Space

Atlantic Ocean

Antarctica

All life-or-death situations

Witness Statements

Some of the witnesses wrote books about their adventures and mentioned these otherworldly experiences.

SOUTH

SHACKLETON

From *South* by Ernest Shackleton:

"During that long and racking march of thirty-six hours over the unnamed mountains and glaciers of South Georgia, it seemed to me often that we were four, not three."

From *Sailing Alone Around the World* by Joshua Slocum:

"Looking out of the companionway, to my amazement I saw a tall man at the helm."

Main theories

Our brains can conjure up an extra "person" as a way of helping us to cope in difficult times. It is a **SURVIVAL MECHANISM** sometimes called **THIRD MAN SYNDROME.** (Although in Shackleton's case it was a fourth man!)

Neuroscientists (brain scientists) have done experiments with people to see if they can make them feel as if another person is with them. They have done this by stimulating certain parts of the brain.

In times of danger and trouble, helpful ghosts visit us. It could be spooky but is instead rather comforting.

Does this mean our brains switch on a kind of "autopilot" in times of stress and danger? We think we are hearing and feeling another person, but it is coming from within ourselves.

Slocum might have been delirious with fever and imagined it all.

Lindbergh was very tired, which could have made him imagine voices.

Ghostly Word

specter

Another word for a ghost, phantom, or apparition.

Deep-Sea Monsters

For as long as people have sailed the seas, there have been tales of gigantic monsters or sea serpents that rear up out of the waves. Are we any closer to finding out what might be lurking in the depths?

In 1848, HMS *Daedalus* was sailing in the South Atlantic Ocean when Captain Peter M'Quhae and six of his crew spotted an enormous creature swimming past the ship.

The mysterious beast was about 60 feet (18 meters) long with a large, snakelike head that it held high above the waves. The monster was dark brown with a yellowish-white throat, and seemed to have a kind of shaggy mane along its back.

Sketch of the Brazil sea serpent drawn by a witness.

In 1905, two members of the British Royal Zoological Society reported another strange sighting off the coast of Brazil. They saw a large fin or frill sticking out of the water, with a great big head and neck in front of it. They could also see an enormous body under the water.

San Francisco Bay also seems to have something mysterious living in the water. On February 5,1985, brothers Bill and Bob Clark spotted a 60 foot (18 meter) long, snakelike beast chasing seals. It was moving its body up and down, making humps visible above the water. They could also see its yellow underbelly and a fan-shaped fin.

The Legendary Kraken

Kraken is the name given to a terrifying sea monster that makes an appearance in many traditional old tales of the sea. Is it possible that a kraken exists in real life?

In March 1941, a group of British sailors was on a life raft in the South Atlantic Ocean. They were attacked by jellyfish and sharks, but worse was to come. An enormous creature rose up out of the depths, grabbed a sailor in its powerful tentacles, and dragged him into the sea.

This scary monster and the kraken of the stories might be some kind of gigantic squid. These deep-sea creatures do exist, although not much is known about them. They have huge grasping tentacles and arms equipped with suckers and hooks. They definitely sound like the sort of squid that would have *you* for dinner!

Turn over to read the **case file** notes . . .

CASE FILE: Deep-Sea Monsters

The evidence so far . . .

Turn back to read the stories behind the case file.

Location

All the world's oceans and seas.

Witnesses

Hundreds of people over hundreds of years

sailors scientists fishermen

Can they all be imagining things or lying?

M'Quhae Witness Statement

"It had no fins, but something like a mane of a horse, or rather a bunch of seaweed, washed about its back."

When the story was published in the newspapers people said it must have been an elephant seal. M'Quhae said he knew the difference between a large seal and this weird beast.

Clark Brothers' Evidence

Blurry Video

Does it show sea serpent humps, or are those just seabirds sitting in the water?

Bill Clark says, "I don't care if anyone believes me. I know what I saw."

Identikit

- Makes series of humps when moving.
- Humps go up and down and NOT side to side like a snake.
- Long, snakelike body.
- Frilly fin that looks like a mane.
- Dark color with light underbelly.

Seems not to harm humans, unlike the kraken!

People are mistaking creatures like whales, eels, seals, sharks, or oarfish for sea serpents. Oarfish can grow up to 36 feet (11 meters) long.

Sea serpents might be some sort of animal left over from the ancient past. Perhaps it is a marine dinosaur!

We only know a tiny fraction about life in the oceans, so it is possible that there is an unknown beast like a sea serpent.

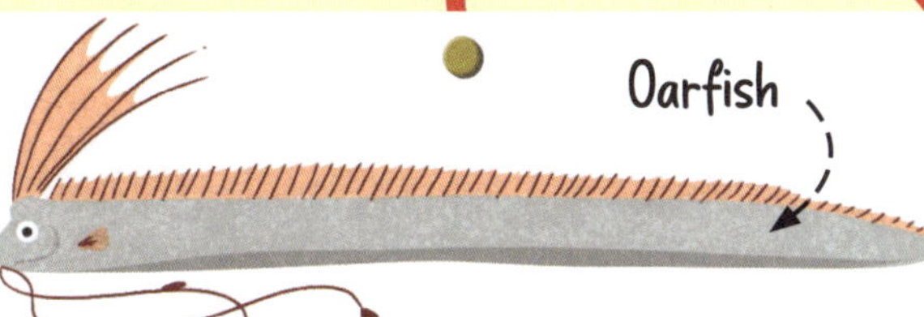

Main theories

The prehistoric **coelacanth** (SEEL-uh-kanth) was thought to have been extinct until a fisherman pulled one up from the depths in 1938.

Nessie's Cousins?

The famous Loch Ness Monster is said to lurk in the extremely deep Loch Ness in Scotland. Many people say they have sighted and even photographed the beast. Some believe it is possible that it is a type of dinosaur called a plesiosaur. Others say that all the photos and sightings are hoaxes.

Nessie may not be the only lake-lurking monster in the world!

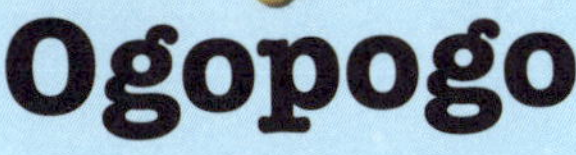

Mokele Mbembe

Lives in the swamplands of the Congo in Africa.

Strange dinosaur-like creature that seems to also be able to walk on land.

Selma

Lives in Lake Seljordsvatnet, Norway.

A black humpbacked creature with a long body. Underwater sonar equipment has detected moving objects that may be 60 feet (18 meters) long.

Ogopogo

Lives in Lake Okanagan, Canada.

In 1974, a vast undulating creature in the water bumped into a swimmer.

Beastly Word

undulating

Moving like a wave, either up and down or side to side.

DEEP-SEA MONSTERS

Fire from Within

John Irving Bentley was a retired doctor living in Pennsylvania. He was last seen alive on December 4, 1966. The next morning a gas utility worker named Don Gosnell let himself into Mr. Bentley's house to read the meter in the basement. He had a key because Mr. Bentley was elderly and disabled.

Don Gosnell was surprised to see a pile of ash in the basement. As he went upstairs he noticed a light blue haze of smoke in the house and a sickly, sweet smell.

In the bathroom he was horrified to see the burned remains of Mr. Bentley. All that was left of him was a bit of right leg with the slipper still on the foot. Mr. Bentley's walker was lying across a huge hole burned in the floor directly above the basement and the pile of ash. The rest of the room was strangely undamaged.

For centuries there have been stories of humans suddenly bursting into flames for no apparent reason. The name given to this mystery is **spontaneous human combustion**, or SHC. The victim's body, or most of it, is completely burned up. A sticky pile of ash is left behind, but the surroundings are hardly damaged.

In 1725, a woman named Nicole Millet was found burned to death in Reims, France. The chair she was sitting in was untouched by the fire. Madame Millet's husband was charged with murder. Luckily for him, a doctor thought there was something odd about the case and managed to convince the court that she had been a victim of spontaneous human combustion.

In 1731, an elderly Italian countess died in a sudden fire that did not damage the room she was in. All that was left of Countess Bandi were her legs and three fingers. The nineteenth-century English writer Charles Dickens was so intrigued by this story that he included a case of SHC in his novel *Bleak House.*

Cases of SHC are very rare, but as recently as 2010, an elderly man in Ireland died in such mysterious circumstances that investigators eventually chalked it up to spontaneous human combustion.

Turn over to read the **case file** notes . . .

CASE FILE: Spontaneous Human Combustion

The evidence so far . . .

Turn back to read the stories behind the case file.

Key Words

Spontaneous means that something happens without any obvious cause.

Spontaneous human combustion is when a person bursts into flames and the cause cannot be found. The fire seems to come from within the body.

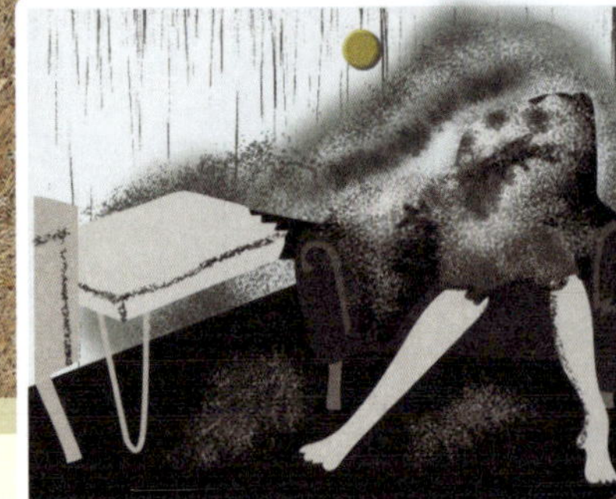

Clues

- Photos of scenes usually show intense incineration of the victim. Nothing but an arm or leg is left.
- The surrounding room and furnishings are often not very damaged.
- In the Bentley case there was a hole burned in the floor. The ash had fallen into the basement below in a neat pile. The fire had not spread.
- In other cases sticky ash was found on furniture.

Witnesses

Usually no witnesses. Victims often on their own in a closed room. This makes it difficult for investigators to know exactly what happened and what started the fire.

Victims

Most victims of SHC are elderly.

The Bentley Case: He was a smoker, but his pipe was found in his bedroom. Could he have dropped burning ash on himself and tried to get water from the bathroom, but fallen and knocked himself out? Maybe the flames then took hold and killed him.

The Wick Effect: The victims may already be unconscious, through illness or too much alcohol. They are too near to the source of a fire, like a cigarette or open fire. The body becomes like a human candle with the fat burning with a slow but intense heat. This is why the ashes are fatty. Don Gosnell described the smell in Bentley's house as "somewhat sweet, like starting up a new oil-burning central heating system."

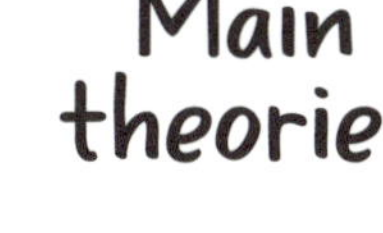

Main theories

Freaky lightning called **ball lightning** strikes a person and incinerates them but does not touch anything else around them.

There is some **unexplained electrical charge** within the body itself that causes it to burst into flames.

There must be some **scientific explanation** for the fire, but the bodies are so badly burned that it is impossible to tell what caused it.

1 Unconscious victim

2 Fat burns in center of body.

3 Body largely consumed by fire.

But why doesn't the fire spread to other parts of the room?

Fiery Word

incineration
When something burns to ashes.

Astonishing Superpowers

Is it possible for some people to have astonishing paranormal powers?

Walking on Fire

Every May there is a festival in northern Greece and southern Bulgaria. As part of the celebrations people walk barefoot across a layer of burning wood.

This is just one of many religious ceremonies around the world during which people walk across burning coals or wood without harming themselves.

The Hindu festival of Thimithi includes walking across a firepit.

On the Indonesian island of Bali young boys and girls perform a sacred dance called Sanghyang around and across a fire.

Bending Spoons

In the 1970s a man named Uri Geller became very famous for seeming to be able to bend spoons and other metal objects without using any force.

Audiences would watch him gently stroking a spoon and be amazed to see the handle bend.

Many other people claim that they can create similar paranormal effects, using the power of their minds.

Superpower Word

paranormal

Something that does not have an obvious scientific explanation.

Finding Water

Looking for water using a technique called dowsing has been done for thousands of years. Dowsing is also used to search for buried metals, oil, and even missing people.

The searchers, or dowsers, use a special tool. This is often a forked wooden stick called a dowsing or divining rod. The dowser holds the forked end of the rod with one fork in each hand.

The dowser then walks around the search area until the end of the rod twitches and dips down. The more it moves, the nearer the dowser is to what they are looking for.

Seeing the Future

Some people claim they have a "sixth sense" that allows them to see into the future, often in their dreams. This mysterious ability is also called extrasensory perception or ESP.

President Abraham Lincoln is said to have had a dream in which he foresaw his own death. A few days later, on April 14, 1865, he was shot during a visit to the theater. He died the next day.

After the tragic sinking of the ocean liner *Titanic* in 1912, many people said that they had had premonitions that there would be a disaster. Some even refused to sail on the ship at the last minute.

Turn over to read the **case file** notes . . .

CASE FILE: Superpowers

The evidence so far . . .

Turn back to read the stories behind the case file.

Fire Walking

Theories

* People can walk over fire and hot coals and wood because they are in a state of mind where they feel no pain.

* The feet do not conduct (or carry) heat very well, so if you keep moving, there is not much risk of getting burned.

* The layer of ashes over the hot coals or wood helps to stop too much heat being transmitted into the feet.

It is possible to snuff out a candle with a quick pinch of the fingers without being burned.

DO NOT TRY THIS AT HOME!

NEVER PLAY WITH FIRE OR CANDLES.

Spoon Bending

Theories

* Some people can manipulate (bend or move) solid objects using only the power of their minds. **Psychokinesis** is the word used to describe this ability.

* It is a very clever trick or illusion practiced by magicians.

If you hold a spoon by its neck and quickly tilt it backward and forward, it can look as if the spoon is bending. You can see videos on the internet of how to do this.

Finding Water

Theories

* Dowsers have magical powers that make their rods or sticks twitch.

* Dowsers are tuning into a special force that makes their muscles twitch, thus moving the rod.

* Dowsers are picking up clues in the environment that help them detect the most likely places to find what they are looking for.

Rhabdomancy is another name for dowsing with rods.

Seeing the Future

Theories

* Some people would say **ESP,** or **extrasensory perception,** is a special ability to predict what will happen in the future, but scientists have not been able to prove it exists.

* In Lincoln's case, like many people in important positions, he would have known he was in danger of assassination.

* The *Titanic* was the biggest liner ever built at that time and so people might well have felt nervous about how safe it was.

Superpower Word

premonition

A strong feeling that something (often something unpleasant or horrible!) is about to happen.

Superpower Word

parapsychology

The study of mental abilities that cannot be explained by what scientists know about nature and the world.

Psychic Detectives

Psychometry is the name given to the ability to detect information about someone by touching objects that belong to them. Psychometrists say they can hold an object owned by a missing person to sense what has happened to them.

Cryptic Crop Circles

Patterns in the Fields

In 2001, an amazing pattern appeared overnight in a field at Milk Hill in the county of Wiltshire in the UK. It was nearly 900 feet (265 meters) across, with 409 circles in a fantastic spiral. Who or what made it, and why was it there?

This crop circle was one of many mysterious designs that have appeared in fields all over the world. The crops are usually not cut, but instead carefully flattened to make all kinds of shapes and patterns.

These intriguing formations only appear during the growing season of the crops. Although they are found in many other countries, most of them occur in the UK in Wiltshire. They have even been seen very near to the ancient stone circle of Stonehenge.

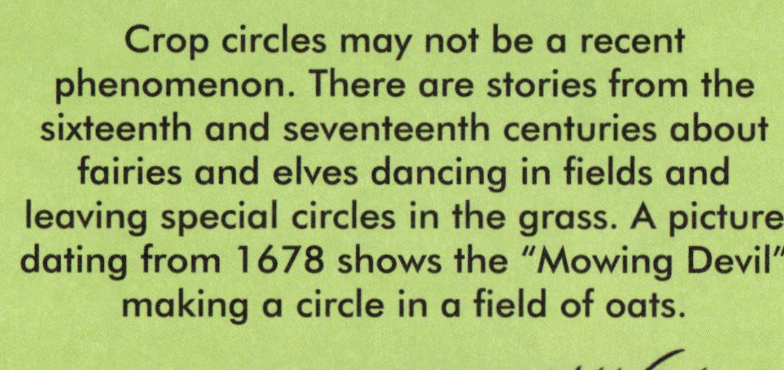

Crop circles may not be a recent phenomenon. There are stories from the sixteenth and seventeenth centuries about fairies and elves dancing in fields and leaving special circles in the grass. A picture dating from 1678 shows the "Mowing Devil" making a circle in a field of oats.

Circles in the Ice

In North America, northern Europe, and Russia, people have spotted mysterious circles in frozen rivers and lakes. Some have been seen on ice that would be too thin for anyone to stand on.

Ice can naturally make circular patterns where water has been moving, but some of these circles have appeared in still water.

In July 1880, a science journal called *Nature* published a letter from a scientist who had found several circular areas of flattened wheat on a farm in southern England. He suggested they were caused by "some cyclonic wind action."

Since the 1990s, the patterns have become more complicated and include huge, intricate geometrical patterns. Whoever or whatever is making them is very good at math, as they are precisely designed and made.

Intriguing Word

phenomenon

Something that you can see exists or happens, but that is unusual or can be hard to explain.

Turn over to read the **case file** notes . . .

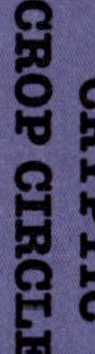

CASE FILE: Crop Circles

The evidence so far . . .

Turn back to read the stories behind the case file.

Description

Swirling circular shapes or more complex designs including triangles and interlocking forms.

The average size of a crop circle is around 200 to 300 feet (60 to 90 meters) in diameter. The Milk Hill circle is extra large.

Time

Whoever or whatever is making them usually does it at night.

Location

Seen around the world but mainly in the southern county of Wiltshire, UK.

Photographic Evidence

Many photos exist of these circles. However, the only videos of them being made were filmed by people who later admitted to faking them!

Chief Suspects

In September 1991, two British men, Doug Bower and Dave Chorley, said they had made all the crop circles in England using a plank of wood, a ball of string, and a wire eyepiece attached to a baseball cap! They admitted they had been inspired by the story of a crop circle discovered by a farmer in Australia.

Main Theories

HOWEVER, these circles would be very complicated to make accurately overnight and in the dark. There are also just too many crop circles for them all to have been made by hoaxers.

Some witnesses say that these circles appear over invisible energy lines in the landscape called LEYLINES. They believe that these leylines under the earth connect ancient sites like Stonehenge and the pyramids of Egypt.

They are landing sites for alien craft or messages from extraterrestrials.

They are caused by freaky weather. Small whirlwinds might make the circle patterns. However, could they really make such complicated designs?

UFO Suspects

In September 1974, a farmer from Saskatchewan in Canada reported seeing five small gray domes hovering over his crops. As they rose into the sky, a blast of mist flattened the field into strange "swirled" circles, leaving the rest of the field untouched. Other cases have also been reported. Some people have heard odd buzzing noises or even seen strange lights over fields where crop circles have then been discovered.

CEREOLOGY is the name given to the study of crop circles.

Further Investigation

Farmers may give you permission to visit their crop-circle fields.

Could the causes of ice circles be similar?

The Missing Lighthouse Men

In December 1900, a newly built lighthouse on a remote Scottish island was the scene of a mystery that has never been solved.

On the night of December 15, 1900, an American ship was passing Eilean Mor, the biggest of the Flannan Isles. The captain noticed that there was no light coming from the lighthouse. He reported this, but bad weather from December 17 and onward stopped anyone from sending a boat out to investigate until the December 26. Assistant lighthouse keeper Joseph Moore was on board the *Hesperus* as it approached Eilean Mor.

There was no reply to the ship's whistle and no one came to greet them at the landing platform. Moore ran up to the lighthouse and hammered on the door. Three lighthouse keepers should have been on duty, but no one answered. Nervously, he opened the unlocked door and stepped inside.There was absolutely no sign of life inside the lighthouse: the clock had stopped, the beds were unmade, but the kitchen was neat and tidy. Most puzzling of all, the light seemed to be in perfect working order.

As Moore looked around he noticed that one set of oilskin waterproofs had been left hanging in the hallway. Where were the other two sets, and where on earth were the three lighthouse men?

The crew of the *Hesperus* searched the island. On one of the landing platforms a box used for storing ropes had completely disappeared, leaving only a tangled mass of rope.

An enormous piece of rock had also been dislodged from the cliff above. But, lower down, a crane used for unloading boats was unharmed.

On December 29, Superintendent Robert Muirhead of the Northern Lighthouse Board arrived on Eilean Mor to conduct his own investigation. He was disturbed to read some odd entries in the lighthouse log.

The log entry for December 12 said that a huge storm with severe winds was raging around the island. Strangely, it also noted that one of the men, Donald McArthur, had been crying.

The log for December 13 said the weather was still terrible and that the men were praying. This was odd because the bad weather had not started until December 17.

The final log entry was on the morning of December 15. It stated:

"Storm ended, sea calm. God is over all."

So what could have happened to the three lighthouse keepers of the Flannan Isles after this final log entry?

Turn over to read the **case file** notes . . .

CASE FILE: Flannan Isles Disappearances

The evidence so far . . .

Turn back to read the story behind the case file.

Location

The Flannan Isles are seven small, rugged islands off the coast of the Hebridean island of Lewis in Scotland.

TIMELINE OF EVENTS

December 15: No light from lighthouse reported by a passing ship.

December 17–25: Bad weather prevents anyone going to investigate.

December 26: Lighthouse Board boat *Hesperus* makes it to the island. No sign of the three lighthouse men.

December 29: Superintendent Muirhead visits. Reads mysterious entries in log.

There was no radio or phone contact in those days.

The Victims

James Ducat, principal keeper

Thomas Marshall, second assistant

Donald McArthur, occasional keeper

Main Theory

Two of the lighthouse men went out to mend some storm damage. The third man observed a huge, freak wave coming toward them. He rushed out to warn them. All three were swept out to sea.

Clues

* Gate and doors neatly shut but left unlocked.
* Everything tidy indoors, and the light is primed for use.
* One of the three sets of oilskins is left indoors.
* Massive damage to some of landing stage area.
* Crane is undamaged.
* Lighthouse logbook contains weather reports and comment on McArthur being upset.

Beware False Evidence!

Over the years this sad story has grabbed people's imagination. Poems, songs, and even an opera have been written about the mystery. Very strange theories have been dreamed up, including the magical transformation of the men into massive black seabirds!

Many Unsolved Questions . . .

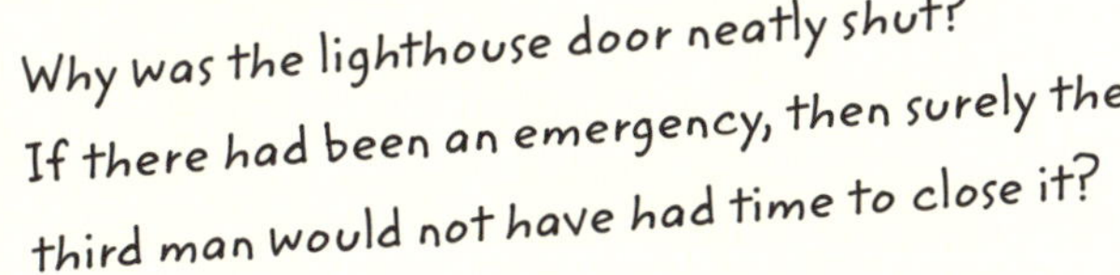

Why was the lighthouse door neatly shut? If there had been an emergency, then surely the third man would not have had time to close it?

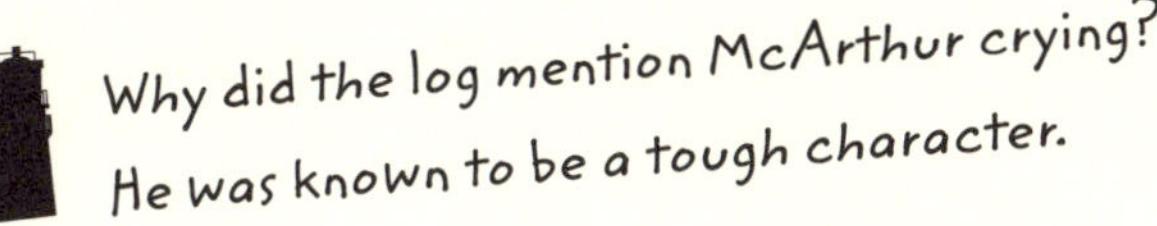

Why did the log mention McArthur crying? He was known to be a tough character.

Why did the weather reported in the log not match the weather elsewhere? The storms did not start until December 17.

Was the landing stage damaged before or after December 15?

Why were no bodies ever washed ashore?

FURTHER DISAPPEARANCES TO INVESTIGATE

The *Mary Celeste*: A ship discovered drifting with no sign of its crew in 1872.

The vanishing soldiers: An entire battalion of British soldiers disappeared without trace in 1915 during a First World War battle at Gallipoli in Turkey.

The mystery of the Bermuda Triangle: An area of the Atlantic Ocean where planes and boats mysteriously disappear.

Mystery Word

inexplicable
Something that is impossible to explain.

PART 2
REAL-LIFE DISASTERS
INVESTIGATE WHAT REALLY HAPPENED!

DISASTER DOSSIER
Real-Life Disasters

When we hear about disasters, we feel scared. It is only natural to feel this way. The idea of being in a disaster ourselves is terrifying! That is why it is so important to understand how disasters have happened, and to find out how they can be prevented in the future.

Read the incredible stories of the disasters in the following pages, then look at the DISASTER DOSSIER for each. You will be able to examine the facts behind what really happened and follow in the footsteps of the experts who investigate and try to predict or prevent disasters.

Disasters can be natural or human-made. Examples of natural disasters are earthquakes, volcanic eruptions, and hurricanes. Human-made disasters happen because of something humans have done.

Investigating and understanding

After a disaster, experts are called in to investigate what has happened and why. This can take many years of gathering evidence and talking to survivors. These experts might include volcanologists who study volcanoes, meteorologists who track the weather, and historians who look into disasters of the past.

Experts also try to predict when natural disasters are going to happen. This can save many lives, but you will see that some disasters are easier to predict than others. Perhaps you will want to become one of these experts yourself?

After human-made or natural disasters, new rules are often made to keep people safe. For example, children in some countries learn at school how to survive an earthquake or a tornado.

Eyewitness statements

Disaster investigators must always be very careful to interview the people who have been through a disaster or witnessed one. They may find out vital clues about what happened and why. What questions would *you* ask?

Locations

The maps on the dossiers will show you where these disasters happened. Are some places in the world more likely to experience disaster than others?

Disaster Word

There is a full list of the disaster words and other related terms on the final page of this book.

perilous

annihilate

FURTHER INVESTIGATIONS

You might think of another disaster to investigate. You could even write your own DISASTER DOSSIER!

The Unsinkable *Titanic*

On April 10, 1912, the majestic *Titanic* set sail on her first ever voyage from England to New York. She was not only the largest steamship in the world at that time but also one of the most luxurious. For the passengers traveling in first class, there were elegant cabins and dining rooms, and a beautiful, sweeping staircase with gold-plated crystal lights. Such a ship seemed unsinkable!

As the *Titanic* was crossing the Atlantic Ocean on Sunday, April 14, the captain began to receive messages from other ships in the area. They warned him to beware of icebergs, but Captain Smith decided not to slow down.

At 11:40 that night, one of the sailors on lookout duty spotted an iceberg! He quickly rang the warning bell. First Officer William Murdoch gave the order to steer away from the berg and to put the engines into reverse.

But it was too late! Seconds later the iceberg ripped into the hull of the ship and water began to pour in. By midnight, the captain gave the order to launch the lifeboats. Families were split up as women and children were given places in the boats first.

Just after two o'clock in the morning, the terrified passengers on the lifeboats watched in horror as the stern (back) of the ship reared high into the air. Hundreds of people still clinging to the ship fell into the ocean to die of hypothermia in the freezing water. Finally, the huge ship broke in half and then plunged beneath the waves.

Hours later the cold, exhausted survivors were rescued by another ship, the *Carpathia*. On board, a lucky few were reunited with loved ones they thought they had lost forever. But two-thirds of the people on board the *Titanic* had died. How could such a magnificent, "unsinkable" ship have come to such a tragic end?

Turn over to read the **disaster dossier** . . .

TITANIC DISASTER DOSSIER

Turn back to read the story of the disaster.

Location

Timeline of sinking

April 14 11:40 p.m.	Iceberg spotted by lookout. Collision with berg.
April 15 12:45 a.m.	Lifeboats launched.
April 15 2:18 a.m.	Bow (front) of ship sinks underwater. Ship breaks up.
April 15 2:20 a.m.	Stern (back) rises up into air. *Titanic* sinks completely.
April 15 4:10 a.m.	First lifeboats seen by *Carpathia*.
April 15 8:30 a.m.	Last survivors rescued by *Carpathia*.

DEATHS AND SURVIVORS

No one knows the exact number of people who were on board the *Titanic*.

* Some people with tickets may not have turned up for the trip.

* Maybe there were a few stowaways!

* About 1,500 people died.

* 706 were rescued.

Eyewitness statements

"The boats were being only partly filled, their capacity being about 65 and they were being loaded with about 30 or 40 people.

"I saw the masses of people who had backed steadily toward the stern of the big ship as her nose slowly sank fall into the ocean as the vessel went up on end and disappeared beneath the water."

John B. Thayer Jr., who jumped into the ocean and was pulled onto an overturned lifeboat

"An officer was shouting, 'Come on here, lively now, this way, women and children,' and before I knew what was happening we were in a lifeboat . . . while the men stood back serious and sober, watching us."

Mrs. Wells, a passenger in second class

TITANIC SINKING
NO LIVES LOST

April 16th 1912
TITANIC DISASTER GREAT LOSS OF LIFE

Some newspapers got it wrong!

Why did so many people die?

* There were not enough lifeboats for everyone.

* Lifeboats were launched before they were full.

* There was no lifeboat drill. Passengers did not know what to do.

* Only one ship came to the rescue.

Investigating and understanding

Design of the ship

* The hull had 16 compartments. There were dividing walls called bulkheads between each one. The shipbuilders said the ship would not sink, even if four compartments were flooded.

* BUT five of the compartments were damaged by the collision AND there were gaps at the top of the bulkheads. Water flooded over them, like an over-full ice cube tray.

Speed and steering

* The US Senate held an inquiry and blamed Captain Smith for ignoring iceberg warnings and steaming ahead through the icefield.

* The ship was so huge that it took too long to steer away from the iceberg.

Saving lives

In 1913, new rules were made at the International Conference for Safety of Life at Sea.

INTERNATIONAL CONFERENCE FOR
SAFETY OF LIFE AT SEA
• 1913 •

*There **MUST** be a lifeboat space for every passenger on a ship and lifeboat drills on every voyage.

* There **MUST** be a 24-hour radio watch to make sure distress signals are always picked up by other ships in the area.

* An International Ice Patrol was set up. This patrol still warns ships of icebergs in the North Atlantic today.

FOLLOW THE EXPERTS

STRANGE STORIES

After the disaster, stories were told about people having premonitions or foreseeing the disaster. Some even said the ship had been cursed.

Evidence from the wreck

* In 1985, oceanographer and deep-sea archaeologist Robert Ballard found the wreck of the *Titanic*.

* Instead of one big hole in the hull, scientists saw several thin gashes. It also looked like the metal plates of the hull had split apart.

* Examination of metal samples showed that the metal used was not strong enough to stand up to an icefield full of icebergs.

Disaster Word

hypothermia

This is when you get so cold it can kill you. The icy water where the Titanic sank caused death within 15 to 30 minutes.

A Quaking Planet

The ground we walk on looks solid, but there are many places on our planet where the earth sometimes shakes and causes terrible disasters. In 1906, a huge earthquake shook the city of San Francisco, California. People were peacefully sleeping in their beds when their homes began to shake violently.

Chimneys crashed down from rooftops, houses crumpled, and all the church bells in the city started to clang. People were trapped inside falling buildings and many were killed. Gas pipes ruptured and fires broke out. The city began to burn in a terrible fire that lasted for three days. Over half of the people in the city lost their homes. It is hard to know just how many people died in the disaster, because even the records at City Hall were destroyed.

Fires often break out after earthquakes and make the disaster even worse. But these are not the only dangers. Sometimes an earthquake creates giant waves, or tsunamis, which sweep away buildings and people.

On November 1, 1755, the people of Lisbon, Portugal, were in church to celebrate the Feast of All Saints. At around nine o'clock in the morning a huge earthquake shook the city. Everyone rushed out of the churches and cathedrals, which were crashing down all around them. They dashed down to the shore, where they thought they would be safer.

Strangely, the sea had drawn back from the coast. The Lisbon townspeople were astonished to see old shipwrecks and fish flapping about on the seabed. They didn't know that this meant they were in deadly danger. Within minutes, a giant tsunami thundered in and swept thousands of people away. Huge waves battered not only Portugal, but also Spain and North Africa.

In Japan, an earthquake caused not only a series of tsunamis but also massive landslides. The Great Kanto Earthquake of 1923 destroyed the cities of Tokyo and Yokohama and the surrounding countryside. A whole mountainside collapsed. It pushed an entire village, including a station and a train full of passengers, into the sea.

Earthquakes can devastate huge areas and kill thousands of people. Can these disasters ever be predicted?

Turn over to read the **disaster dossier** . . .

EARTHQUAKE DISASTER DOSSIER

Turn back to read the story of the disaster.

Locations

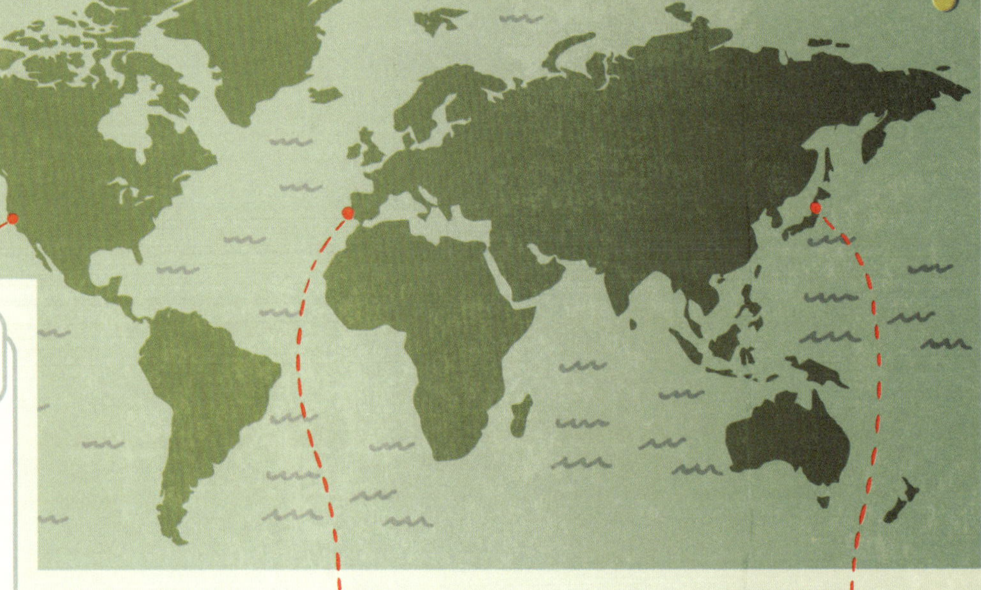

San Francisco Quake

Date:
April 18, 1906

Deaths:
At least 3,000 people killed

"I heard a low distant rumble. It was coming from the west, louder and louder. . . . Then it hit. Power and trolley lines snapped like threads. The ends of the power lines dropped to the pavement not 10 feet from where I stood, writhing and hissing like reptiles. Brick and glass showered about me."

Thomas Jefferson Chase, ferry ticket clerk

The Call=Chronicle=Examiner
SAN FRANCISCO, THURSDAY, APRIL 19, 1906
EARTHQUAKE AND FIRE: SAN FRANCISCO IN RUINS

Lisbon Quake

Date:
November 1, 1755

Deaths:
Up to 60,000 people killed (in Portugal and also Spain and Morocco)

"This dismal earthquake had such an influence upon the sea and river, that the water rose, in about ten minutes, several yards perpendicular . . . with a cry that the sea was coming in, all people crowded forward to run to the hills."

British merchant's letter to his brother

Great Kanto Quake

Date:
September 1, 1923

Deaths:
At least 140,000 people killed

"To stand or walk was a physical impossibility. Those who did not crouch in terror the instant the shock began were thrown violently to the ground. The earth split and cracked in all directions."

W. D. Cameron, Canadian businessman in Yokohama

Why does the earth shake?

The Earth's surface is made of huge slabs of rock called tectonic plates. These are constantly moving. An area called a fault line is formed where two plates slip past each other.

Sometimes the edges of two plates in a fault line get stuck as they are trying to slide past each other. They keep trying to move and this stores up energy in the rock edges.

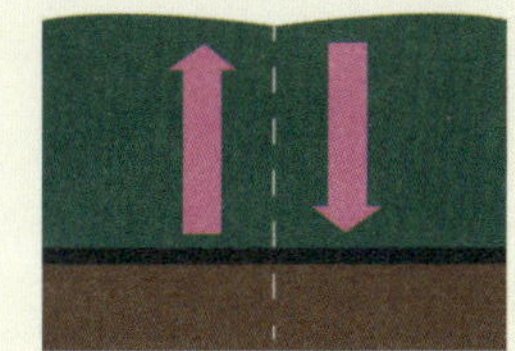

When the plates finally "unstick," the stored energy spreads out in shock waves called seismic waves. They shake the earth!

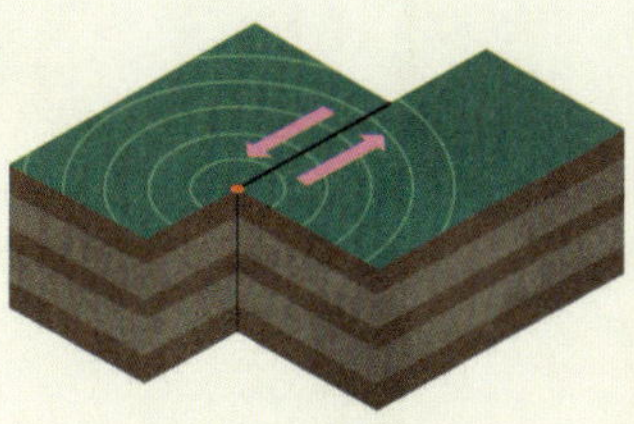

Investigating and predicting

* Seismologists are scientists who study earthquakes. They use special instruments called seismometers to measure the shock waves from earthquakes.

* Seismometers record even the smallest earthquakes all over the world. There are about 500,000 detectable earthquakes every year!

* Scientists also track the movements of tectonic plates using GPS (Global Positioning System). They monitor fault lines and build up a picture of where most earthquakes seem to happen and how powerful they are.

BUT . . .

It is impossible to predict exactly WHEN there will be a major earthquake.

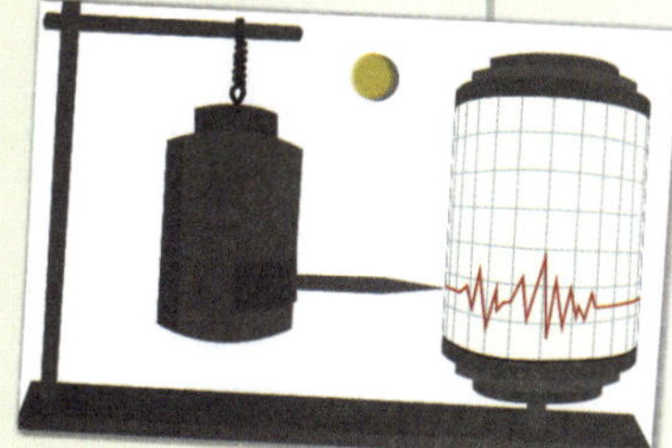

Saving lives

* Earthquakes smash down buildings and kill many people. As the world's population grows, more and more people will be living in earthquake zones. Buildings must be built to sway instead of fall down during a quake.

* Schoolchildren in parts of the world where there are earthquake risks often practice a special earthquake drill.

DROP! COVER! HOLD ON!

* If you are outside: get away from buildings, streetlights, and overhead wires.

FOLLOW THE EXPERTS

Disaster Word

devastate

To cause great harm or destruction.

Tsunami danger!

* Sometimes there are earthquakes under the oceans. These can cause massive waves of water called **tsunamis** (soo-na-mees). Seismologists have set up warning systems in some parts of the world. If an underwater quake is detected, they can warn people to get to safety before a tsunami hits.

Life-saving facts

* In 2004, there was a terrible tsunami in Southeast Asia. A young girl named Tilly Smith was on a beach when she saw the sea was pulling very far out from shore. She had just learned about tsunamis at school. She knew that as a tsunami wave reaches the shore it grows higher, but the trough before the wave pulls water away from the shore first. Tilly shouted to everyone to run away from the beach before the big wave arrived. She saved many lives that day.

Dino Disaster

Dinosaurs lived happily on Earth for more than 100 million years. Most of them died out suddenly about 66 million years ago. Even though this is a very, very, *very* long time ago, scientists think they may know how nearly all the dinosaurs were wiped out.

There is a gigantic crater on the coast of Mexico. It was made by a monster rock from outer space crashing into the surface of our planet. It must have been a terrifying sight. As it smashed into Earth, the impact made giant clouds of ash and dust fly up into the atmosphere. These blotted out the light from the sun for years. The planet became dark and cold.

Plants and trees need sunlight to grow. Without sunlight they die, and no new plants or trees grow either. The poor vegetarian dinosaurs (herbivores) would have had nothing left to eat. They would have starved to death. At first, the meat-eaters (carnivores) would have eaten all the herbivores, but soon there would have been no food for them to chomp on either! It was a disaster for the dinosaurs.

But this is not the only mega-rock to have landed on Earth from space. In the Arizona desert, there is another enormous crater. You could fit nearly three Empire State Buildings end-to-end across it. Scientists think it is about 50,000 years old.

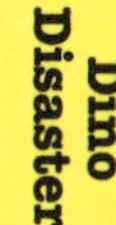

In 1908, a mysterious object exploded in the skies above Siberia in Russia. It is such a remote area that there were not many people living there. The closest people to the explosion were some reindeer herders. They were in their tents about 20 miles (30 km) away and were blown into the air and knocked unconscious. The forest around them burst into flames and many reindeer died. People who lived hundreds of miles away saw a huge fireball in the sky and heard deafening bangs.

There are thousands of rocks whizzing around in space, but luckily, big ones do not smash into Earth very often. In 1996, one of them missed our planet by only 280,000 miles (450,000 km). This sounds like a long way away, but it is not much further than from here to the moon. We don't want to end up like the poor old dinosaurs!

Turn over to read the **disaster dossier** . . .

SPACE ROCK DISASTER DOSSIER

Turn back to read the story of the disaster.

Locations

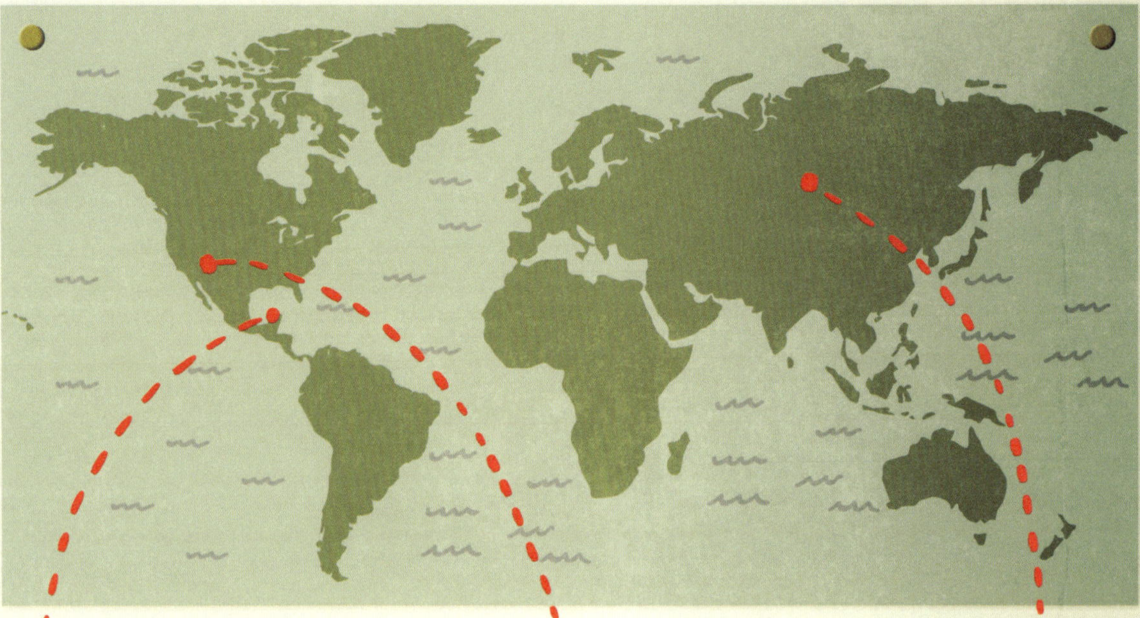

Dinosaur Killer Rock

Chicxulub, Yucatan Peninsula, Mexico

Space rock landed:
Between 65 and 66 million years ago

Size of crater:
112 miles (180 km) wide

NO HUMAN WITNESSES

Arizona Mega-Rock

Winslow, Arizona, USA

Space rock landed:
50,000 years ago

Size of crater:
4,000 feet (1,200 meters) wide

NO HUMAN WITNESSES

Siberian Fireball

Tunguska, Siberia, Russia

Date of explosion
June 30, 1908

Size of crater:
No crater but massive destruction of forest

Eyewitness statements

"Everything around was shrouded in smoke and fog from the burning fallen trees. . . . Many reindeer rushed away and were lost."

Reindeer herder, Siberia

"High above the forest the whole northern part of the sky appeared covered with fire. . . . At that moment there was a bang in the sky, and a mighty crash. . . . The crash was followed by a noise like stones falling from the sky, or guns firing."

Witness, 37 miles (60 km) away

What are space rocks?

* **Asteroids** are made of rock. They can be hundreds of miles across or as small as pebbles.

* **Comets** are balls of ice, rock, and dust with long tails of gas and dust. They can be the size of a small town!

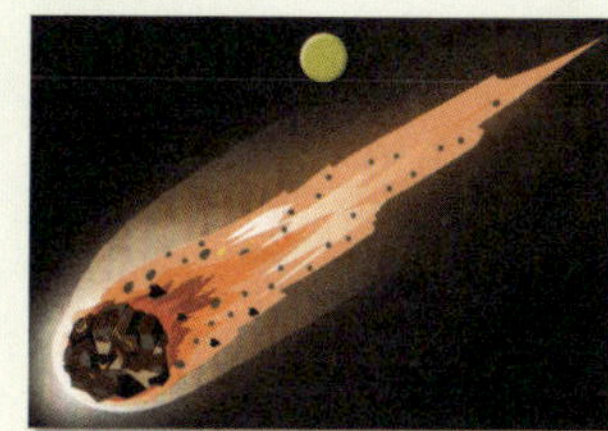

Investigating and understanding

* Fossil scientists (paleontologists) have worked out that most of the dinosaurs became extinct around 66 million years ago. Scientists who study the rocks on Earth (geologists) say the Chicxulub Crater in Mexico was made by a large asteroid or comet around the same time.

* Geologists have also discovered a metal called iridium in rock layers dating from 66 million years ago. Iridium is very rare on Earth, but it IS found in space rocks. When the Chicxulub space rock exploded on Earth's surface it would have covered a huge area with iridium.

* Other scientists think that the disaster was not only caused by a space rock. There were also lots of disastrous volcanic eruptions on Earth at around that time.

Predicting and preventing

* Astronomers are scientists who study space. Some of them watch the skies for big asteroids and comets that might come too close to Earth. Luckily for us, these are quite rare!

* Scientists are experimenting with ways of stopping a very large rock from smashing into our planet. One idea is to use rockets to knock the asteroid into a different path, or orbit, so that it does not threaten Earth.

FOLLOW THE EXPERTS

Disaster Word

extinction

This means dying out completely. If a species of animal is extinct, it means there is not one left alive in the whole world.

STRANGE STORIES!

Some people say that the Tunguska fireball was an alien spaceship coming to land on Earth! But scientists believe it was an asteroid that exploded in Earth's atmosphere. That is why people saw a burning ball of fire in the sky.

The Bermuda Triangle

The oceans of the world are huge and beautiful. Many ships and planes travel across them every day. Most of them cross safely, but oceans can also be dangerous places. There is one area of the Atlantic Ocean where many ships and planes have disappeared. In 1964, a journalist named Vincent Gaddis invented a name for this area. He called it the Bermuda Triangle and said that there was something strange and mysterious about these disasters.

An American ship, the USS *Cyclops*, is just one of the many lost ships. In March 1918, the *Cyclops* was carrying a heavy cargo when it set off from Barbados in the Caribbean. It was heading across the Atlantic Ocean toward Baltimore on the East Coast of the United States. Somewhere in the Triangle, disaster struck. The *Cyclops* never reached its final destination, and the huge ship and over 300 crew and passengers were never seen again. There was no call for help from the *Cyclops*, and no wreckage has ever been found.

In 1945, five American Navy bomber planes set off on a training flight from their base at Fort Lauderdale in Florida. At first, everything went well, but then the planes seemed to lose their way. "I don't know where we are," said one of the pilots over his radio. The pilot in charge of the mission also reported, "Both my compasses are out and I'm trying to find Fort Lauderdale."

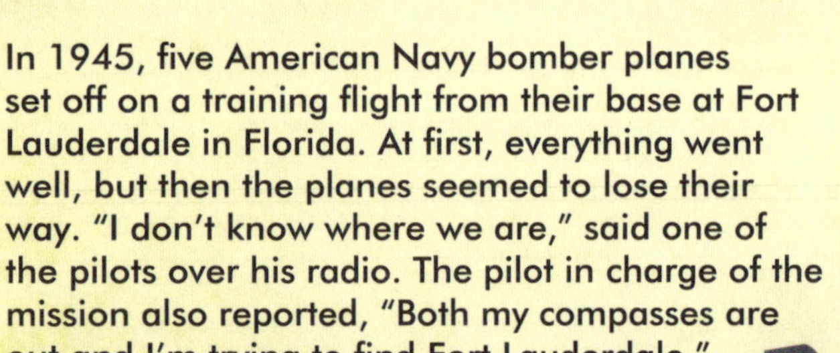

The confused pilots carried on flying and the planes began to run out of fuel. Back at base, no one could understand why the planes seemed to be heading further and further out across the ocean. The Navy urgently sent search planes to look for the missing aircraft. To everyone's horror, one of these rescue planes also disappeared over the ocean. The six planes had vanished with all of their crew.

Other people have somehow survived strange events in the Bermuda Triangle. In 1964, pilot Chuck Wakely saw a dazzling glow around his plane just before all his instruments malfunctioned. Another man, Gerald Hawkes, said the plane he was on suddenly dropped down and then shot up again on the way to the small island of Bermuda. And in 1966, a tugboat was going from Puerto Rico to Fort Lauderdale when its compass and electric power stopped working. The captain said a strange darkness came down and the waves were really high. These experiences must have been terrifying.

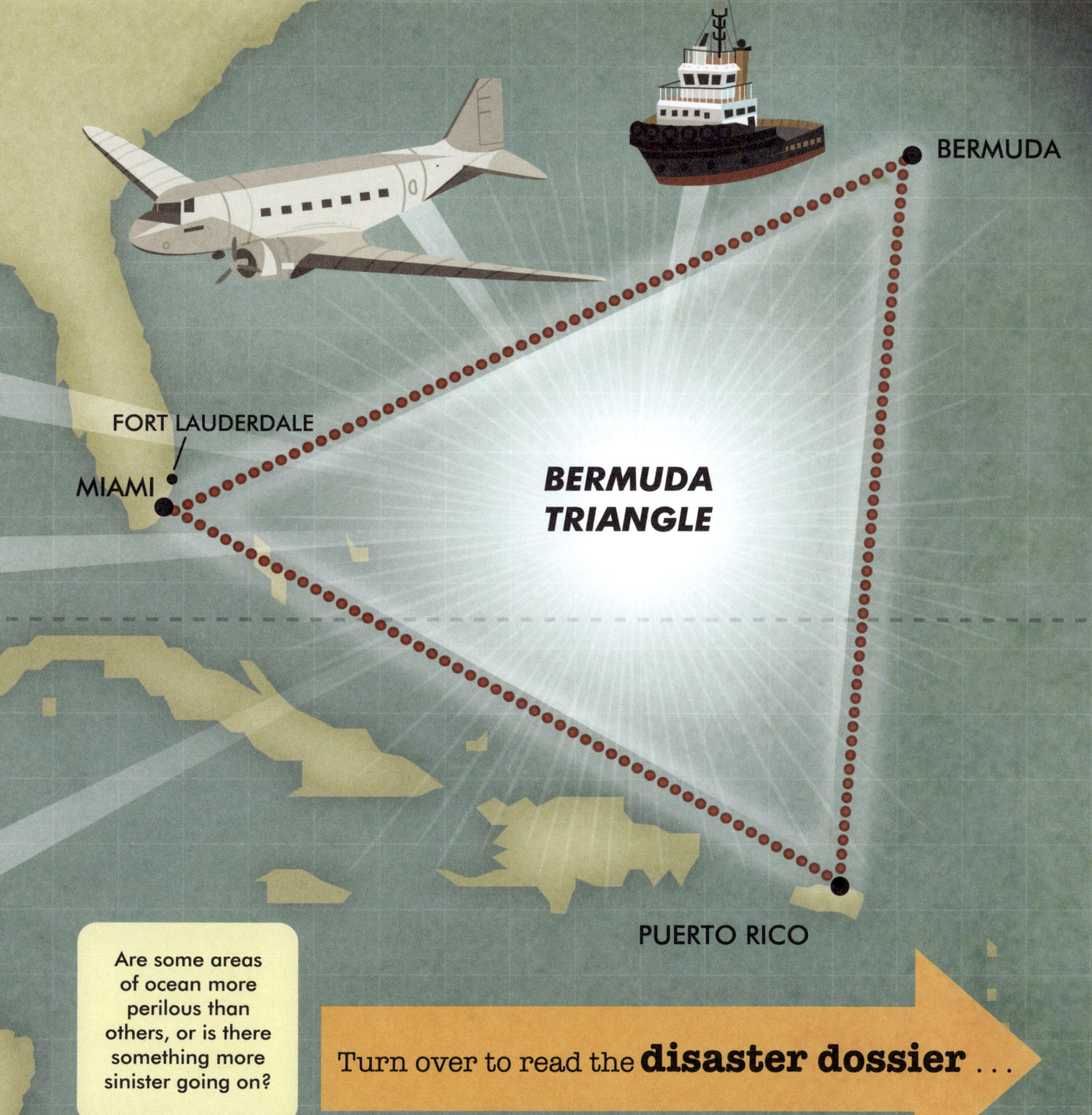

Are some areas of ocean more perilous than others, or is there something more sinister going on?

Turn over to read the **disaster dossier** . . .

TRIANGLE DISASTER DOSSIER

Turn back to read the story of the disaster.

Location

MISSING IN THE TRIANGLE

About 50 ships and 20 planes.
Up to 1,000 people.
The exact number is not known.
NO WRECKAGE EVER FOUND!

Reports of unexplained disappearances started in the 1800s.

A Vanishing Ship	The Lost Planes	Missing Rescue Aircraft
Name: USS *Cyclops*	**Name:** Flight 19	**Name:** Mariner flying boat
Number of crew and passengers: 309	**Number of planes:** 5	**Number of crew:** 13
Date disappeared: Sometime after March 4, 1918	**Number of crew:** 14	**Date disappeared:** December 5, 1945
	Date disappeared: December 5, 1945	

Eyewitness statements

"It was as if a giant hand was holding the plane and jerking it up and down . . . time and space seemed to disappear."

Gerald Hawkes, airplane pilot

"The water seemed to be coming from all directions."

Don Henry, tugboat captain

Many books have been written about the Triangle.

What do we know so far?

* The Atlantic Ocean is HUGE. It is very difficult to find wreckage from accidents.

* This means there is no evidence to examine. Without the wreckage of the ships and planes, it is hard to investigate why they went down.

* There are many theories behind the disappearances. No one knows for sure!

Investigating and understanding

Theory: Nothing unusual here!

* The US Coast Guard says there is nothing strange about the number of planes and ships going down. There are often very bad storms in the area. It is also very busy with a lot of ocean traffic.

* The *Cyclops* was overloaded. It probably sank in a massive storm.

* The US Navy said that the planes of Flight 19 got lost for "reasons unknown." The fuel ran out and the planes crashed into the ocean.

* The search plane crashed, because its fuel tank exploded. Some oil slicks on the ocean were spotted at the time. These could have been from the plane.

Theory: Human error?

* Compasses do not point to the geographical north at the North Pole. They point to magnetic north. The difference between these two directions depends on where you are in the world. Sailors and pilots must take this into account.

* Some of the planes and boats that have disappeared may have been steered by people who did not have the skills to find their way, or to survive such a wild and stormy ocean.

Weirder theories

Rogue waves

* Oceanographers (scientists who study the oceans and seas) believe that unusually high waves can appear out of nowhere in the middle of the ocean. These freak waves can be over 100 feet (30 meters) high and could easily destroy a ship.

Gas bubbles

* There is a lot of methane gas under the seabed. Could giant bubbles of gas sink ships and stop aircraft instruments from working properly? If so, this would be happening in other areas of the oceans too.

Strange glow

* Some kinds of seaweed give off an eerie glow at night. They are covered in bioluminescent bacteria. Could this have caused the odd light effects seen by Chuck Wakely?

Disaster Word

perilous

Extremely dangerous

STRANGE STORIES!

Vincent Gaddis and the authors of many other books on the Triangle believe there is something supernatural about the disappearances. Others say there are alien spaceships under the ocean that are capturing the planes and ships, along with their crews.

Inferno at Sea

We use a huge amount of oil and gas to power our planet, and some of it is found under Earth's seas and oceans. Enormous platforms, or rigs, are used to drill and pump out these fossil fuels. The people who work on these rigs get there by helicopter. The rigs pump night and day, so staff work in shifts around the clock.

The Piper Alpha platform was 120 miles (190 km) off the coast of Scotland in the wild and windy North Sea. In 1988, it was the scene of the world's worst-ever oil rig disaster. Oil rigs can be dangerous places, but no one expected such a terrible tragedy.

Piper Alpha was built to pump oil, but by the 1980s it was also pumping gas. It was connected to other rigs in the North Sea by a network of pipes. On the night of July 6, 1988, one of Piper Alpha's pumps stopped working. The night shift workers switched on another pump and there was a sudden explosion! It ripped through the rig and was quickly followed by another deadly blast. A huge fireball whooshed high into the night sky.

Meanwhile, oil and gas were still being pumped along the pipes from the other rigs. These pipes melted and there were more explosions. Fire now spread uncontrollably throughout Piper Alpha. Desperate workers had to save themselves in any way they could. Men leapt into the sea from high up on the rig or scrambled down ropes. Rescue boats came to help and, tragically, one of these was blown up by another explosion.

There were more than 200 men on the rig that night. About 80 of them were off-duty in the accommodation block. They waited to be rescued by helicopter, but it was impossible. There was too much black smoke, and immense flames shot over 650 feet (200 meters) into the sky. Just before midnight the rig began to buckle and groan. The entire accommodation block slid beneath the sea. None of the men inside could be saved.

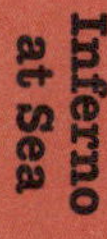

By quarter to one in the morning, all that was left of Piper Alpha was a black burning stump sticking up out of the sea. In just two hours the platform had been destroyed and many men had lost their lives. How could such a terrible disaster have happened?

Turn over to read the **disaster dossier** . . .

OIL RIG DISASTER DOSSIER

Turn back to read the story of the disaster.

Location

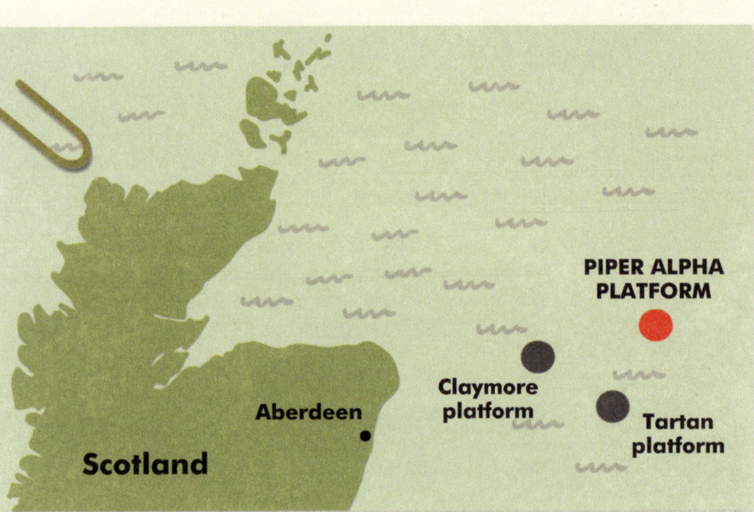

Timeline of disaster

July 6 9:45 p.m. First pump stops working. Second pump switched on.

10:00 p.m. First explosion, quickly followed by another blast.

10:20 p.m. Gas pipes from nearby rigs melt. Another explosion. Fire spreads throughout Piper Alpha.

10:50 p.m. More explosions. Rescue boat destroyed.

11:50 p.m. Four-story accommodation block collapses into the sea.

Eyewitness statements

"The explosion came. Next second, I'm 15 foot away up the other end of the control room."

Geoff Bollands, control room operator, describing the first explosion

"The last time we went to the rig, the whole world seemed to be on fire. The noise was absolutely deafening. If you could imagine a blow-torch and then magnify the sound of that blow-torch maybe three, four thousand times and you will get an idea of the noise."

Charles Haffey, crewman on a rescue boat, who helped to rescue over 30 men (before his boat was snapped in half by an explosion)

"You wonder why people would jump out of a 30- or 40-story block window when fire is at their back. Well, I know why now, because I jumped as well and I was very lucky to survive. When I hit the sea, I went very deep, but you could see above that the flames were lighting up the surface of the sea."

Roy Carey, instrument technician, jumped from a height of over 70 feet (20 meters) into the sea

DEATHS AND SURVIVORS

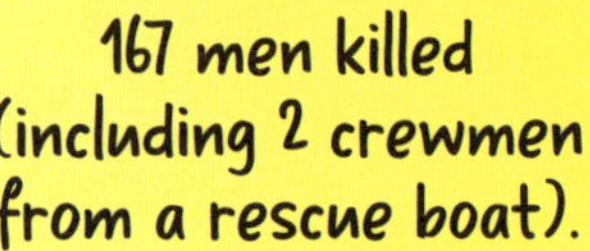

167 men killed (including 2 crewmen from a rescue boat).

61 survivors.

Inferno at Sea

How did the fire start?

* When the first pump stopped working, the second one was switched on. This pump was faulty.
* The night shift did not know that the day workers had not finished repairing it. It should not have been used.
* Gas leaked out and exploded. This was the first explosion.

Investigating and understanding

There was an official inquiry into the tragedy. The experts said:

* There should have been better communication between the day and night workers so that the second pump was not used.

* The rig had been built to pump oil, not gas. It had fireproof walls, but these were not strong enough to stand up to gas explosions. The firewalls were smashed by the blasts and the fire then spread quickly throughout the whole platform.

* The control room was so badly damaged in the first explosion that it was impossible to start the rig's automatic firefighting systems.

* The other connected rigs should have stopped pumping fuel immediately.

* The accommodation block of the platform should not have been built above the pumping area.

Saving lives

* Oil rigs are dangerous places, but the brave people who work on them deserve to be as safe as possible.

* The experts involved in the inquiry came up with 106 urgent changes to make oil and gas platforms much safer in the future.

FOLLOW THE EXPERTS

Heroes of the fire

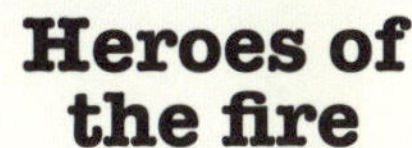

* There were many heroes that terrible night. Twenty men received medals for their bravery in helping others to escape the inferno. Sadly, two of the medals were awarded to the families of men who had given up their own lives to save others.

Disaster Word
inferno

A very large fire that is out of control.

Height of rig = 12 double decker buses

Airship Explosion

Airships were first invented in 1852. They were huge, torpedo-shaped aircraft with a "balloon" full of gas to keep them up in the air. Passengers traveling in comfortable cabins loved the way the airships glided along, lighter than air.

On the evening of October 4, 1930, a huge airship took to the skies above England. The brand-new airship R101 was on its way to India on its first big flight. A crowd of people on the ground cheered as the ship rose into the sky. There were 54 people on board.

The passengers ate their evening meal in the airship's luxurious dining room. Then they strolled around or sat on a special viewing deck to look down below. It was like being on a cruise ship in the sky. By eight o'clock in the evening R101 was flying over London, just below the clouds.

In the days before the journey, some last-minute changes had been made to the design of the airship, but there was not enough time to test the ship at top speed or in bad weather. There were some very important passengers from the British government traveling to India and the government did not want to delay the flight. Everyone was excited about the new ship and wanted to show it off to the world.

As the airship flew on into the night toward France, the passengers went to their cabins to sleep. The weather became very windy and rainy, although weather reports said it would improve. At 2 a.m. the captain went off duty and his second officer took control. Just minutes later the airship suddenly dived down toward the ground. People were knocked off their feet and the furniture slid around.

The crew managed to steady the airship, but it was now flying too close to the ground. It needed to get back up to a safe height. They did all they could, but the airship dived again. The crew knew they would have to make an emergency landing. "We're down, lads," said one of them.

The airship landed safely, and the crew must have been so relieved. Then disaster struck!

The ship exploded into intense flames. Only six people survived the fireball. How could such a tragedy have happened to such a magnificent new airship?

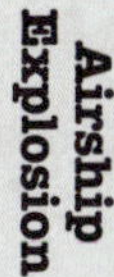

Turn over to read the **disaster dossier** . . .

AIRSHIP DISASTER DOSSIER

Turn back to read the story of the disaster.

Location

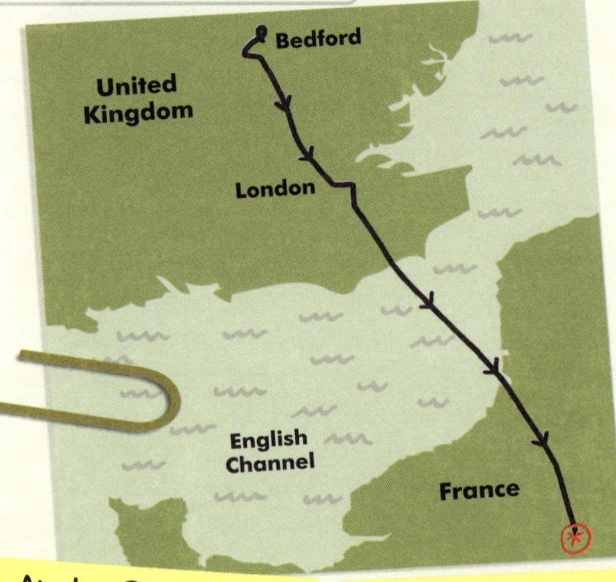

Airship R101 was 3 times as long as a Boeing 747.

The gas in the airship "balloon" was HYDROGEN = highly flammable.

Timeline of flight

October 4 6:36 p.m.	Airship R101 lifts off from Bedfordshire, England.
October 5 2 a.m.	Captain Irwin hands over command to his second officer. Weather is very windy and rainy.
October 5 2:07 a.m.	Airship suddenly dives toward the ground. Crew manage to steady the ship.
October 5 2:08 a.m.	Airship dives down again. Crew crash-lands ship, but seconds later . . . the AIRSHIP EXPLODES INTO FLAMES.

NUMBER OF DEAD

48 people (including 2 who died later in hospital)

Eyewitness statements

"Shock of impact not great – more a crunch than a blow – I was not even shaken. Within 2 seconds of striking, a blinding flash of fire appeared to originate from above the control car. I saw the mass of flame."

Harry Leech, foreman engineer, described the two dives and then the crash-landing. He survived.

"After the explosion the sky was filled with pieces of burning wreckage and these floated away from the spot slowly sinking; it looked like a large firework going off."

Miss Moillez, age 14, French girl who saw the disaster

TERRIBLE AIR TRAGEDY

R101 CRASHES IN FLAMES

ALL AIRSHIP LEADERS LOST

Airship Explosion

Everyone on duty in the control room died. This makes it very hard to know exactly why the accident happened.

What probably happened?

* The bad weather ripped into the front of the ship. Gas leaked out of the gasbags. This made the ship dive down.

* The crew could not stop the airship from losing height. They had to crash-land, nose first.

* The engine twisted round and set fire to the highly flammable hydrogen gas.

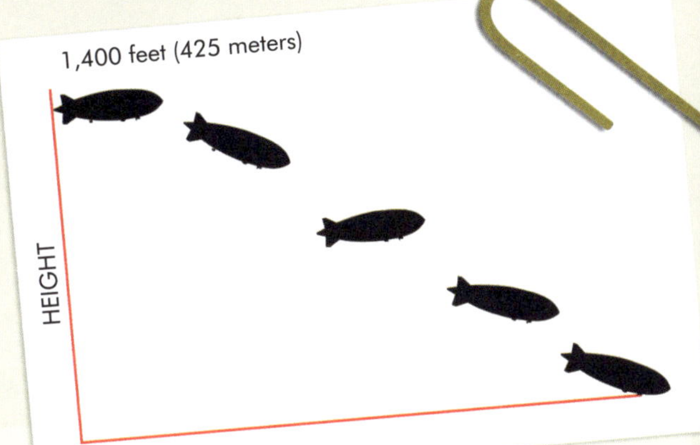

Investigating and understanding

Airship design and testing

* The design was changed to add another gasbag. This was to help the heavy ship lift into the air safely.

* The ship should then have been tested at full speed and in bad weather. This was not done before the flight to India.

* Some parts of the outer cover had been repaired before the flight. They should have been completely replaced instead. The bad weather on the flight split the cover.

Pressure to leave on time!

* The passengers included the British Air Minister, Lord Thomson, and most of the expert engineers who had designed the airship. They had all worked hard to get R101 ready for the flight.

* There were big expectations about the amazing journey so no one really wanted to delay the departure, even though they knew the airship needed more testing.

FOLLOW THE EXPERTS

Wind and rain

* The weather was very stormy, especially in France where the airship went down. The split in the cover would have let in rain. This would make the airship heavier and hard to keep in the air.

* A downward gust of wind may also have forced the airship into the first dive.

Bad timing

* The captain handed over control to the second officer at 2 a.m., just before the first dive. This officer immediately had to deal with the emergency.

Disaster Word
flammable

Something that bursts into flames very easily, like the hydrogen gas in the airship.

STRANGE STORIES

After a disaster like this, people sometimes say they had a feeling that something bad was about to happen. Some of these premonitions can be very spooky. One of the crew members was leaving home for the flight when his little boy began to cry, "I haven't got a daddy." His father did not return.

Wild Weather

Extreme weather causes some of the worst natural disasters in the world. Terrible floods and violent storms can destroy whole towns and kill many people.

Mega-storm

On November 8, 1970, a violent storm began to form over the Bay of Bengal in South Asia. It became a swirling mass of high winds (a cyclone) and it was heading toward the nearest land. Ships sent urgent messages to warn the people living on the coast that there was a terrible cyclone on its way, but many people did not get the warning in time.

The cyclone smashed into the coast of Bangladesh (then called East Pakistan) on November 12, 1970. By now the speed of the wind was a terrifying 115 mph (185 kph). The wind was so strong that it pushed masses of seawater onto the land. Bangladesh is very low-lying, even compared to the normal level of the sea. This storm surge completely inundated islands and land near the coast.

The worst-hit area was a large island called Bhola. Whole villages were swept away. Hundreds of thousands of people and farm animals died in what was called the Bhola Cyclone. It was one of the deadliest cyclones ever.

Monster Twister

Stormy weather can also bring terrifying whirlwinds called tornadoes. Although they do not last for as long as cyclones, they can destroy everything in their path and even suck up water from rivers. They are like a monster vacuum cleaner ripping across the land.

On March 18, 1925, a deadly tornado ripped through three American states. It roared through towns, farms, and even across rivers in Missouri, Illinois, and Indiana. The ferocious, whirling winds obliterated whole towns. Houses blew away, trees snapped, and objects were picked up and then dumped back down many miles away.

The tornado rampaged over a distance of 200 miles (320 km) for three and a half hours. It destroyed several towns, killed hundreds of people, and injured thousands more. The tornado was the largest and longest-lasting tornado in US history.

Turn over to read the **disaster dossiers** . . .

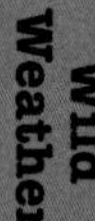

CYCLONE DISASTER DOSSIER

TORNADO DISASTER DOSSIER

Turn back to read the story of the disasters.

Location of Bhola Cyclone

NUMBER OF DEATHS

Up to 500,000 people = half a million. But no one knows exactly how many people died.

Eyewitness statement

"I was clinging to a bamboo pole but a wave swept me out to sea. After six hours, at daybreak, it washed me up 15 miles away. I am the only survivor of my family."

Modan Mohan Shaha, 18 years old

Location of the Tri-state Tornado

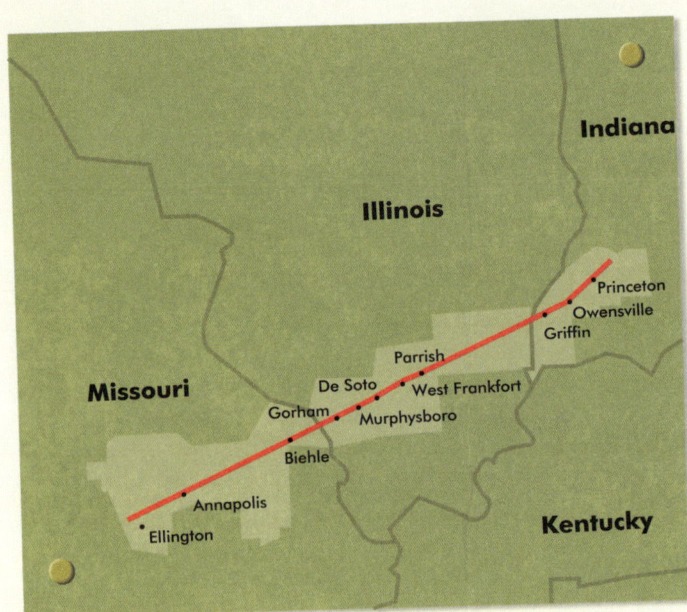

NUMBER OF DEATHS

Nearly 700 people died. 2,000 were injured.

Eyewitness statement

"There was a great roar. Like a train, but many, many times louder. . . . The air was full of everything, boards, branches of trees, garments, pans, stoves, all churning around together."

Judith Cox, who was having lunch in Gorham, Illinois

(A cow even came through the roof of the restaurant!)

What is a cyclone?

* A **cyclone** is a violent storm with very high winds that spiral around a calmer center, or "eye." They form above seas and oceans and can be 250 miles (400 km) wide.

Cyclones are also called hurricanes or typhoons.

What is a tornado?

* A **tornado** is a twisting funnel of air that can form during thunderstorms. It touches down over land and is narrower, faster, and more violent than a cyclone.

Investigating and understanding

* When the Bhola Cyclone happened in 1970 it was very difficult to warn everyone in time. There were no mobile phones in those days.

* In 1925, the word "tornado" was not even in use by American weather forecasters. Additionally, tornadoes were nearly impossible to predict without modern technology.

Saving lives

* Special cyclone shelters have been built in Bangladesh to keep people safer.

* People who live in certain areas of the USA know what they have to do in case of a tornado warning. Their best chance is to shelter in a basement room without windows. You can't outrun a tornado!

FOLLOW THE EXPERTS

Predicting wild weather

* Meteorologists are scientists who study our planet's weather. They use radar networks and satellite pictures to forecast and track storms. Weather warning systems are now used around the world to tell people when cyclones or tornadoes are likely to happen.

Climate change danger

* The climate on Earth is getting hotter and humans are making it worse. Sea levels are rising and even the ice at the North and South Poles is melting. People living in low-lying countries, like Bangladesh, are in even more danger from flooding during wild weather.

Disaster Words

inundate To flood an area with water.

obliterate To destroy completely.

The Halifax Explosion

During the First World War, many ships passed through the huge sheltered harbor of Halifax, Nova Scotia, on the Canadian coast. The ships carried soldiers who were going to battle. They also took essential supplies of food, fuel, and weapons across the Atlantic Ocean to war-torn Europe.

On the morning of December 6, 1917, one of the ships leaving the harbor was a large Norwegian vessel called the SS *Imo*. Its mission was to take urgent supplies to the people of Belgium. That day, another ship was just about to enter the port. It was a French ship called the SS *Mont-Blanc*. It was packed with tons of explosives and was going to join other ships returning to the war in Europe.

The captain of the *Imo* had already waited for several days in the harbor for supplies to be delivered. He set off fast but had to keep changing course to avoid other ships in the busy waterway. Meanwhile, the *Mont-Blanc* was making its way into the harbor through the narrow entrance to the port. It was being steered by Francis Mackey, a harbor pilot.

Mackey was shocked to see the *Imo* speeding straight toward him. Despite both ships sending out warning whistles, it was too late to avoid a collision. The *Imo* gashed a hole in the hull of the *Mont-Blanc*. This started a huge fire in the fuel drums on deck. An enormous plume of black smoke rose up into the sky. People on shore, including many children on their way to school, gathered to watch.

The crew of the *Mont-Blanc* rowed for their lives to shore and tried to tell everyone to run away. By now the burning ship, packed with 3,000 tons of explosives, was drifting toward the busiest part of Halifax. Just after nine o'clock, the *Mont-Blanc* was annihilated in a gigantic, catastrophic explosion.

Hundreds of people died instantly. The shock waves from the explosion shattered windows and doors many miles away. People were blown up into the air and badly injured by shards of glass. Hot gas and shrapnel rained down. Fire raged through the wooden buildings of the city. The blast also created a huge wave that devastated the shore area.

The Halifax Explosion was one of the greatest catastrophes in the history of Canada. How could a city be wrecked like this?

Turn over to read the **disaster dossier** . . .

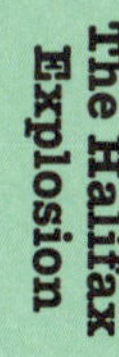

EXPLOSION DISASTER DOSSIER

Turn back to read the story of the disaster.

Location

Timeline of explosion

December 6 7:30 a.m. SS *Mont-Blanc* heads toward the entrance of the harbor. The SS *Imo* is speeding toward the entrance in the opposite direction.

About 8:45 a.m. The ships collide and the *Mont-Blanc* catches fire. The fire burns for 20 minutes. Many people gather on shore to watch.

Just after 9:04 a.m. SS *Mont-Blanc* explodes with devastating force.

Eyewitness statements

"We saw the ship blow up, but I thought the heavens had fallen, I suppose it was because such a terrific cloud had come over. . . . I looked out at the water, and absolutely everything was flying. You could see everything flying into the water."

Dorothy Chisholm, who witnessed the explosion on her way to work that morning

"The town was literally ablaze, the dry dock and dockyard buildings completely demolished and everywhere wounded and dead."

Frank Baker, Royal Navy sailor

"They looked like they were deliberately trying to run into each other. They had room to get by – there was no need of a collision. . . . Suddenly the explosion went off."

Barbara Orr, schoolgirl who saw the collision

THE HALIFAX HERALD

FRIDAY, DECEMBER 7, 1917

HALIFAX WRECKED

DEATHS AND SURVIVORS

Nearly 2,000 dead.

9,000 injured.

1.5 square miles (3.8 square km) of Halifax was flattened.

It was the BIGGEST human-made explosion ever (until the atomic bomb in the 1940s).

Why were there so many deaths and injuries?

* The massive shock waves blasted the buildings and killed at least 1,600 people immediately. The glass in windows bent and shattered, killing and injuring many more.

* A fireball of hot gas and debris shot up into the air and then rained down. Fire spread fast through wooden buildings.

* A huge 52 foot (16 meter) wave washed over the shore area. It spread over three city blocks.

Investigating and understanding

* The disaster happened during the war so at first some people thought that the explosion was caused by enemy spies.

* There were many investigations into the disaster. In 1919, an official inquiry finally decided that the *Mont-Blanc* and the *Imo* were equally to blame.

Dangerous cargo

* A ship carrying explosives should have been flying a red flag to let other ships know it had an extremely dangerous and flammable cargo.

* The *Mont-Blanc* was NOT flying a red flag. This was to avoid being a target for enemy submarines.

* Before the war, a boat with such a lethal cargo would not even have been allowed into the main harbor.

Saving lives

* Before the war, ships leaving the harbor had to give way to ships coming in. But now there were so many ships using the port that it made it harder to stick to this rule.

* Ships leaving the harbor were supposed to keep to the right. The *Imo* was too far left, because it had already had to move out of the way of two other ships in the busy waterway.

* The captain of the *Imo* was in a hurry to get back to deliver essential supplies to Belgium. He was going too fast and he had not let the port authorities know that he was leaving the harbor.

FOLLOW THE EXPERTS

The ships sounded their warning whistles. Neither of them moved out of the way of the other until it was too late.

Could the *Mont-Blanc* have sailed back out again before the 3,000 tons of explosives caught fire? The captain gave the order to abandon ship instead.

Disaster Word
annihilate

To wipe out or destroy completely.

The Killer Lakes

Most natural disasters are caused by volcanic eruptions, earthquakes, floods, and wild weather. But in the beautiful countryside of Cameroon, in Africa, there have been two very mysterious natural disasters.

On the night of August 15, 1984, twelve people were traveling in a truck through an area with many ancient volcanoes. Lakes have formed in some of the old volcano craters and the road went past one of them. Suddenly, the truck stopped and the driver could not start the engine no matter how hard he tried. Everyone inside the vehicle got out. Two people who were sitting on top of the truck watched in horror as all of them collapsed to the ground and died.

Meanwhile, in nearby villages, people were peacefully sleeping. By morning, many families woke up to find that some of their relatives had mysteriously passed away in their sleep. A total of 37 people had now died in a strange and unexplained way. Investigators were puzzled by reports of a light mist in the area. They also saw that the lake, called Lake Monoun, had turned a peculiar rusty color. No one could explain what had happened.

Then, two years later, disaster struck again. This time it happened near another lake in Cameroon, called Lake Nyos. It was a calm blue lake on the side of another old volcano. Many families had lived and farmed for generations in the nearby villages and valleys.

On August 21, 1986, the peaceful lake became a killer. Very few people survived to explain what happened. Villagers were enjoying their evening meals and settling down for the night, when they heard a strange rumbling noise. They were amazed to see a huge spout of water shooting out of their lake. Soon a vast white cloud rose into the air and spread rapidly toward them.

People began gasping for air before collapsing to the ground. All their farm animals fell down too. When a very few people started waking up hours later, they made an appalling discovery. They could not wake other members of their families or their neighbors. They had all died. There was a dreadful silence, because even the birds and insects had been killed. The once-beautiful Lake Nyos had turned a murky red-brown color.

No one had been able to explain the mysterious deaths at Lake Monoun, and now there had been an even more terrible disaster. What had happened to kill so many people and animals?

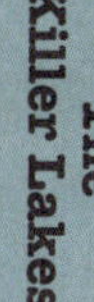

Turn over to read the **disaster dossier** . . .

LAKES DISASTER DOSSIER

Turn back to read the story of the disaster.

Location

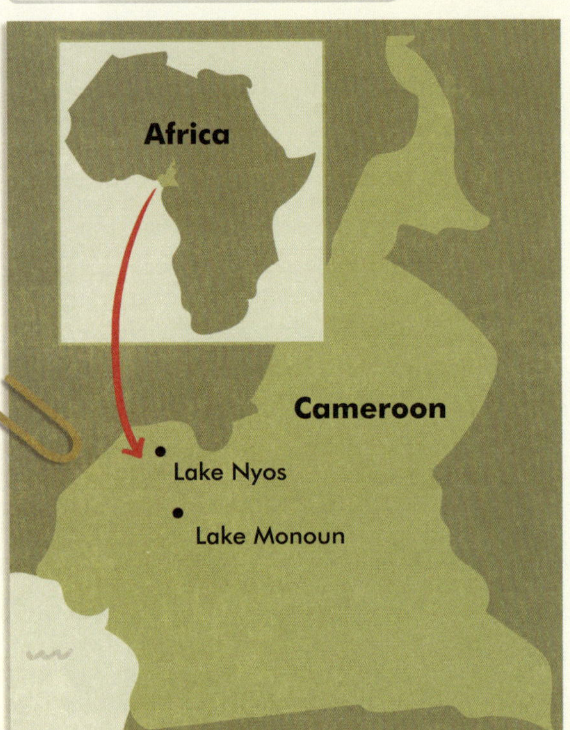

Lake Monoun

Date:

August 15, 1984

Numbers of deaths:

37 people

Lake Nyos

Date:

August 21, 1986

Numbers of deaths:

Over 1,700 people and thousands of cattle

The effects of the disaster spread 16 miles (25 km) from the lake.

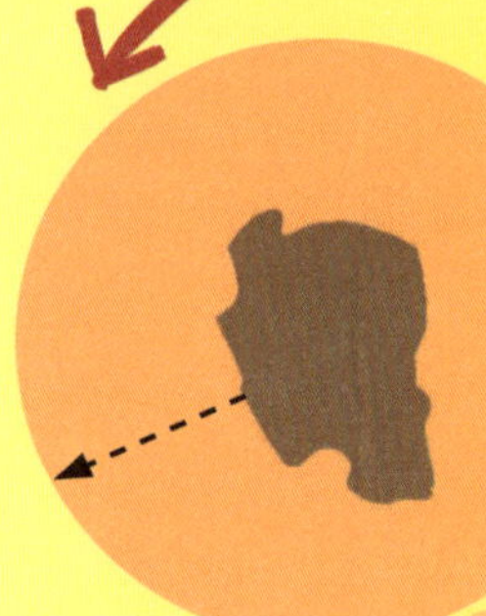

Eyewitness statements

"I heard my daughter snoring in a terrible way, very abnormal. . . . When crossing to my daughter's bed . . . I collapsed and fell. I was there till nine o'clock in the morning . . . until a friend of mine came and knocked at my door . . . I wanted to speak, my breath would not come out. . . . My daughter was already dead.

"I got my motorcycle. . . . A friend whose father had died left with me. . . . As I rode . . . through Nyos I didn't see any sign of any living thing."

Joseph Nkwain, one of very few survivors

"Nine of us survived in my family. . . . It was a stroke of luck that our house was located on a hillside . . . the toxic gas did not completely envelop the hills as it did in the valleys where every living thing was killed."

Che Kamasana Jerome, who was eight years old at the time of the disaster and lost many members of his family

The New York Times

In Cameroon, Scenes of a Valley of Death

What killed so many people and animals?

* The mist from Lake Monoun and the white cloud from Lake Nyos were made of gases. The main gas was carbon dioxide (CO_2).

* People and animals need oxygen to breathe, but the CO_2 was like a suffocating blanket that pushed the oxygen out of the way. It asphyxiated people and animals.

* CO_2 is heavier than oxygen, so it flowed down from the lakes into the villages in the valleys below. The only survivors were people who managed to run to higher ground.

CO_2 bursts out of lake.

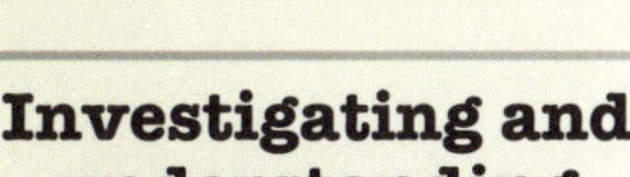

Investigating and understanding

Exploding gas

* Scientists were not quite sure what had caused the deaths at Lake Monoun. After the Lake Nyos disaster they knew that a massive gas eruption must have exploded out of the lakes. It was even powerful enough to change the color of the water.

* Both lakes are in craters left behind by old volcanoes. There is magma (hot liquid rock) deep under these lakes. It leaks carbon dioxide into the water.

* The CO_2 builds up at the bottom of the lakes. The water of the lakes is so calm that the CO_2 does not rise up and bubble away harmlessly. Instead, it builds up like a ticking time bomb waiting for something to trigger it.

But WHY did the gas explode out of the lakes?

"It was one of the most baffling disasters scientists have ever investigated. Lakes just don't rise up and wipe out thousands of people."
George Kling, ecologist

Preventing disaster

* Teams of scientists have put special tubes into both lakes to let the carbon dioxide gas leak out safely. It is like letting the bubbles out of a bottle of soda without it whooshing all over the place.

* BUT experts are worried that the rock walls around Lake Nyos might give way one day. This would not only mean the water would flood out, but it would also let deadly amounts of CO_2 gas burst out again.

FOLLOW THE EXPERTS

Limnic eruption = gas eruption from a lake

* Scientists still DO NOT KNOW what triggered the gas to explode out of the lakes.

* There are several theories. Some geologists (rock scientists) suspect a landslide churned up the water. Others say there was a small volcanic eruption under the lake, or that heavy rainfall disturbed the water.

Disaster Word
asphyxiate
To suffocate or cut off the air we need to breathe.

Mega-Eruption!

Some of the world's worst natural disasters are caused by volcanoes. One of the most destructive eruptions in human history took place on the volcanic island of Krakatau (krak-uh-taow) in Indonesia. There were probably only a few people living on Krakatau, but there were many villages on the neighboring islands of Java and Sumatra.

The year was 1883. For many months, the people living on Java and Sumatra had been disturbed by strange rumbling noises and tremors in the earth.

Then on Sunday, August 26, there was a sudden, sharp explosion on Krakatau. A vast, dark cloud soon covered the island. Before long, the coasts of Java and Sumatra were being pelted with hot ash and there was a fiery red glare over Krakatau. There were more terrifying explosions, and the sea churned and pounded boats in the harbors.

Finally, on Monday morning, Krakatau exploded in a cataclysmic blast. Clouds of gas, rocks, fire, and smoke shot 50 miles (80 km) into the air. The island of Krakatau was almost completely destroyed. The noise from the explosion was the loudest noise EVER recorded! But, most lethal of all, the collapsing island caused terrifying sea waves called tsunamis.

The tsunamis raced along as fast as a speeding car and reached heights of up to 130 feet (40 meters). They smashed into the villages along the coasts of Java and Sumatra and destroyed everything in their paths. By the end of the day more than 36,000 people had died. Most of them were killed by these mega-tsunamis.

The effects of the terrible eruption spread all over the world over the next few months. The volcano had exploded so much ash into Earth's atmosphere that it changed the world's weather and skies. There were fiery-colored sunsets and sunrises, as well as incredible blue, green, and purple light effects. Some sunsets were so vivid that in one American town the fire brigade was called to put out the "fire"!

Krakatau was the first major world disaster to take place after the invention of the electric telegraph. Messages could now be sent all over the world using a network of cables under the seas and over land. It is amazing to think that not only did the effects of the eruption spread around the world, but so did the news of the catastrophe.

Turn over to read the **disaster dossier** . . .

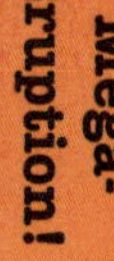

VOLCANO DISASTER DOSSIER

Turn back to read the story of the disaster.

Location

Timeline of mega-eruption

August 26 1 p.m. Sudden large explosion on Krakatau. Black cloud of hot ash shoots up more than 16 miles (27 km).

August 27 5:30 a.m. More massive explosions. Huge waves batter the coasts.

August 27 10:02 a.m. Colossal blast. Ash clouds reach up 50 miles (80 km). Krakatau explodes completely and collapses into the sea. Massive tsunamis follow.

August 27 11 p.m. All is over. Total devastation.

DEATH AND DESTRUCTION

Over 36,000 people killed. 165 villages were obliterated.

Eyewitness statements

"I am writing this blind in pitch darkness. . . . So violent are the explosions that the eardrums of over half my crew have been shattered."

Captain Sampson, from the British ship *Norham Castle* off the coast of Sumatra

"I felt a heavy pressure, throwing me to the floor. . . . Then it seemed as if all the air was being sucked away and I could not breathe."

Mrs. Beyerinck, Ketimbang, Sumatra, describing the effect of the shock waves

"We saw a great black thing, a long way off, coming toward us. It was very high and very strong, and we soon saw that it was water. The people began to run for their lives."

Man who was working in the rice fields of Java

BY TELEGRAPH.

BLOTTED OUT.

Whole Villages Buried.

Mountains Submerged and Islands Made Deserts.

PEOPLE ARE KILLED

GREATEST HORROR IN THE HISTORY OF MODERN TIMES.

Towns and Villages Overwhelmed by the Lava or the Sea.

Thousands of Lives Destroyed - the Eruption Still in Progress.

Earth's surface is like a massive jigsaw made of pieces of rock called tectonic plates. They are constantly moving and there is a thick liquid of hot, melted rock called magma under them.

Why did it happen?

The most violent volcanic eruptions, like Krakatau, happen when one plate is pushed under another.

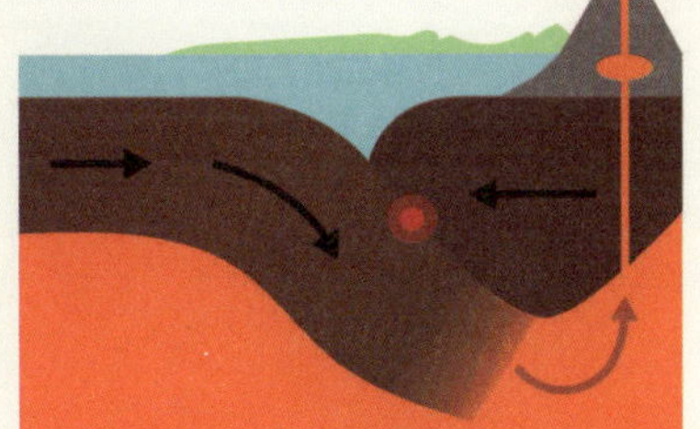

A **tsunami** (soo-na-mee) happens when a large amount of water is suddenly moved by an eruption or earthquake. When Krakatau exploded it caused huge tsunamis that raced across the sea to swamp other islands.

FOLLOW THE EXPERTS

Investigating and understanding

Weird light effects

* These were caused by ash particles in the Earth's atmosphere.

* Meteorologists (scientists who study the weather) realized that there must be air currents carrying the ash around the planet.

* They called it the Equatorial Smoke Stream. Now we know it as the jet stream. It is like a high-speed river of air that affects climate and weather.

Sound and shock waves

* Sounds make air molecules vibrate and change air pressure. An extremely loud sound pushes the air itself, making a shock wave that can burst your eardrums.

* The shock waves made by Krakatau spread out across the world like ripples of pressure. Scientists measured them using instruments called barometers.

* The waves were even detected as far away as London and North America. From this, the scientists understood just how loud the explosion had been.

Predicting blasts

* Volcanologists are scientists who study volcanoes. They try to predict when and how volcanoes will erupt.

* They look at the history of a volcano to see when it has erupted in the past.

* They take samples, record volcano temperatures, and check vibrations (seismic activity) within a volcano.

Disaster Word

cataclysmic

Something that is violently destructive.

BABY VOLCANO WARNING!

Krakatau itself was destroyed in 1883, but in 1926 a new volcano called Anak Krakatau (which means "child of Krakatau") appeared above the waves. It is growing fast and growling already!

The Black Death

Sometimes disasters come in the form of dreadful, killer diseases. If they spread quickly across many countries they are called **pandemics.**

In the fourteenth century, there were many trading routes between the different countries of the world. Merchants brought goods from China all the way to Europe and the British Isles. In October 1347, some trading ships arrived in Sicily from Asia. Sadly, everyone on board was desperately ill or already dead. Their bodies were covered in horrible black blotches.

The sick traders and sailors were not allowed to come ashore, but no one could stop the ships' rats from scampering off into the port. They carried the disease with them. Soon, the people of Sicily were ill and dying too. The illness then spread in a deadly wave across Europe and North Africa.

The disease caused terrible black **buboes** (swellings) and fever. Sufferers coughed up blood and most victims died within days of falling ill. There was no known cure. By 1351, tens of millions of people had died. Whole communities were decimated, leaving behind abandoned buildings and empty "ghost" villages.

People at the time did not know what caused the illness. They blamed all sorts of things like bad smells or being cursed by enemies. Modern historians call this pandemic the Black Death or the Bubonic Plague because of the horrible black buboes. But writers at the time called it the Great Pestilence.

Over the centuries, there were many other outbreaks of the same frightening disease. In 1665, it struck London and killed many thousands of people. Victims were shut up inside their homes and red crosses were painted on the door with the words "Lord have mercy upon us." People still thought the disease might be carried through "bad air," so they smoked tobacco to stop the badness getting into their lungs. Even children were told to smoke!

In the 1860s, the disease appeared again in China. Over the following years, it spread as far as the USA. Sadly, this pandemic killed millions of people before doctors finally began to understand more about it.

Diseases like this can cause terrible disasters, so it is critically important for us to discover as much as we can about them.

Turn over to read the **disaster dossier** . . .

BLACK DEATH DISASTER DOSSIER

Turn back to read the story of the disaster.

Location and timeline of disease

1347 Trading ships arrive in Messina, Sicily, with dead and dying passengers.

1348 Disease spreads through Italy, Spain, France, and North Africa. It arrives in Dorset, England, on a ship from France.

1349 Disease continues to spread throughout Europe. It reaches Wales, Ireland, and the north of England.

1350 Disease reaches Scotland and Scandinavia.

1351 End of the first wave of the Black Death.

Eyewitness statements

"Those who fell sick of a kind of gross swelling of the flesh lasted for barely two days. . . . It generated such horror that children did not dare visit their dying parents, nor parents their children, but fled for fear of contagion as if from leprosy or a serpent."

John of Fordun, fourteenth-century Scottish writer

"People lay ill little more than two or three days and died suddenly. . . . He who was well one day was dead the next and being carried to his grave."

Jean de Venette, French friar who wrote about the Black Death

"And finally it spread over all England and so wasted the people that scarce the tenth person of any sort was left alive."

Geoffrey the Baker, fourteenth-century English writer

NUMBER OF DEATHS

1347–1351
The Black Death killed at least one-third of the population of Europe.

1665
100,000 people died in London
=
one-fifth of the city's population.

Late 1800s
10 million people died in China, India, and the USA.

What IS this disease and what CAUSES it?

MOST LIKELY CAUSE
A type of plague called BUBONIC PLAGUE.

* The rats from the trading ships had fleas on them. The fleas carried a bacterium called *Yersinia pestis.*

* The fleas bit humans and the bacteria got into their blood. This caused swellings called buboes (along with the other symptoms). That is where the name "bubonic plague" comes from.

BACTERIA are tiny, invisible organisms.

BUT some experts think the terrible disease may have been caused by a virus (another kind of germ), and not the plague bacterium.

Investigating and understanding

Digging up the past

* Historians piece together what happened during the Black Death by looking at all kinds of evidence. They read old documents written at the time and search for eyewitness descriptions.

* Archaeologists have dug up pieces of pottery from ancient trash dumps in villages. They can tell if they were thrown away before or after the time of the Black Death. They count the pieces, and from this figure out how many people were alive to use the pottery before and after the pandemic.

Disease ID

* The bacterium that causes bubonic plague was found in 1894 by a French Swiss doctor named Alexandre Yersin and a Japanese doctor, Kitasato Shibasaburo. It was named *Yersinia pestis* after Yersin.

* Epidemiologists are scientists who study what causes diseases and how they spread. They have tested the bones and teeth of Black Death victims from burial pits and found *Yersinia pestis.*

Preventing pandemics

* Modern medicines, like antibiotics, are used to cure cases of plague now. In earlier times, doctors tried some very weird treatments—and they also wore strange outfits to try to avoid catching it themselves!

* Nowadays, there are ways of controlling rats and fleas to prevent them from passing on harmful bacteria to humans.

* Health organizations, like the World Health Organization (WHO), work very hard to treat and prevent the spread of dangerous diseases.

Scary beak mask worn by doctors in the 1600s.

FOLLOW THE EXPERTS

* All of this research is so important because it helps us to understand the way the disease spread across countries. This knowledge can help to protect us in the future.

Disaster Word
decimate
To kill or destroy a large part of something.

MYSTERY & DISASTER GLOSSARY

Annihilate: To wipe out or destroy completely.

Apparition: The strange and unexpected appearance of someone or something.

Asphyxiate: To suffocate or cut off the air we need to breathe.

Bacteria: Tiny, invisible organisms that can cause diseases.

Buboes: Painful swellings on the thighs, neck, armpits, or groin. They are a symptom of bubonic plague.

Cataclysmic: Something that is violently destructive.

Cereology: The name given to the study of crop circles.

Cryptozoology: The study of mysterious animals that may or may not exist.

Decimate: To kill or destroy a large part of something.

Devastate: To cause great harm or destruction.

Extinction: This means dying out completely. If a species of animal is extinct, there is not one left alive in the whole world.

Extrasensory perception (ESP): A special ability to know something without using one of your five senses. One type of ESP is to predict what will happen in the future.

Flammable: Something that bursts into flames easily. (Confusingly, *inflammable* means the same thing! The opposite of *flammable* or *inflammable* is *non-flammable.*)

Hypothermia: This is when you get so cold it can kill you.

Incineration: When something burns to ashes.

Inexplicable: Something that is impossible to explain.

Inferno: A very large fire that is out of control.

Inundate: To flood an area with water.

Leyline: An invisible energy line in the landscape believed by some people to connect ancient sites like Stonehenge and the Great Pyramids.

Megalith: A massive stone used as a standing stone or part of stone circles by prehistoric cultures.

Obliterate: To destroy entirely.

Objective: Making decisions based on facts, not on feelings or beliefs.

Obliterate: To destroy completely.

Pandemic: An outbreak of disease that spreads across many countries or even the whole world.

Paranormal: Something that does not have an obvious scientific explanation.

Parapsychology: The study of mental abilities that cannot be explained by what scientists know about nature and the world.

Perilous: Extremely dangerous.

Phenomenon: Something that you can see exists or happens, but that is unusual or can be hard to explain.

Premonition: A strong feeling that something (often something unpleasant or horrible!) is about to happen.

Pseudoscience: Theories about the world that are not based in science.

Psychokinesis: The ability to move or bend objects using the power of the mind.

Psychometry: The ability to detect information about someone by touching objects belonging to them.

Rhabdomancy: Another name for dowsing with rods, or divining.

Specter: Another word for a ghost, phantom, or apparition.

Spontaneous human combustion (SHC): When a person bursts into flames and the cause cannot be found.

Supernatural: Something that cannot be explained by what we know about the world around us.

Third man syndrome: A phenomenon where people report feeling an unseen presence or spirit offering comfort in life-or-death situations.

Tsunami: A massive, deadly wave created when a huge amount of water is suddenly moved by a volcanic eruption, earthquake, or explosion.

UFO: Stands for Unidentified Flying Object, many of which people believe are alien spaceships.

Ufology: The study of unidentified flying objects (UFOs).

Undulating: Moving like a wave, either up and down or side to side.